Fundu Lagoon

Anish Kapoor

Ellis Flyte   Brian Henson   Marcus Lewis   Alex Lewis

THIS IS FUNDU LAGOON

Fundu Lagoon is a rare, magical destination. Each season both new and returning guests arrive on the remote, dreamy shores of Pemba Island and drift into the gentle rhythm of Fundu life.

Mornings spent idling along the beach in sunshine morph seamlessly into poolside lunches. Dive trips segue into sundowners at the jetty bar and convivial dinners slip effortlessly into late drinks with new friends.

However, the intoxicating easy atmosphere is perhaps more akin to that found in theatre. Beneath the calm surface beats the strong heart of a vibrant and dynamic community.

This book charts the unique inspiration and motivation that built Fundu Lagoon. It touches on the triumphs and travails experienced in constructing a privately owned boutique hotel on a remote equatorial tropical island.

Ultimately, this is a story about the extraordinary people who created the place, those who work in it and those who are lucky enough to visit.

This is Fundu Lagoon.

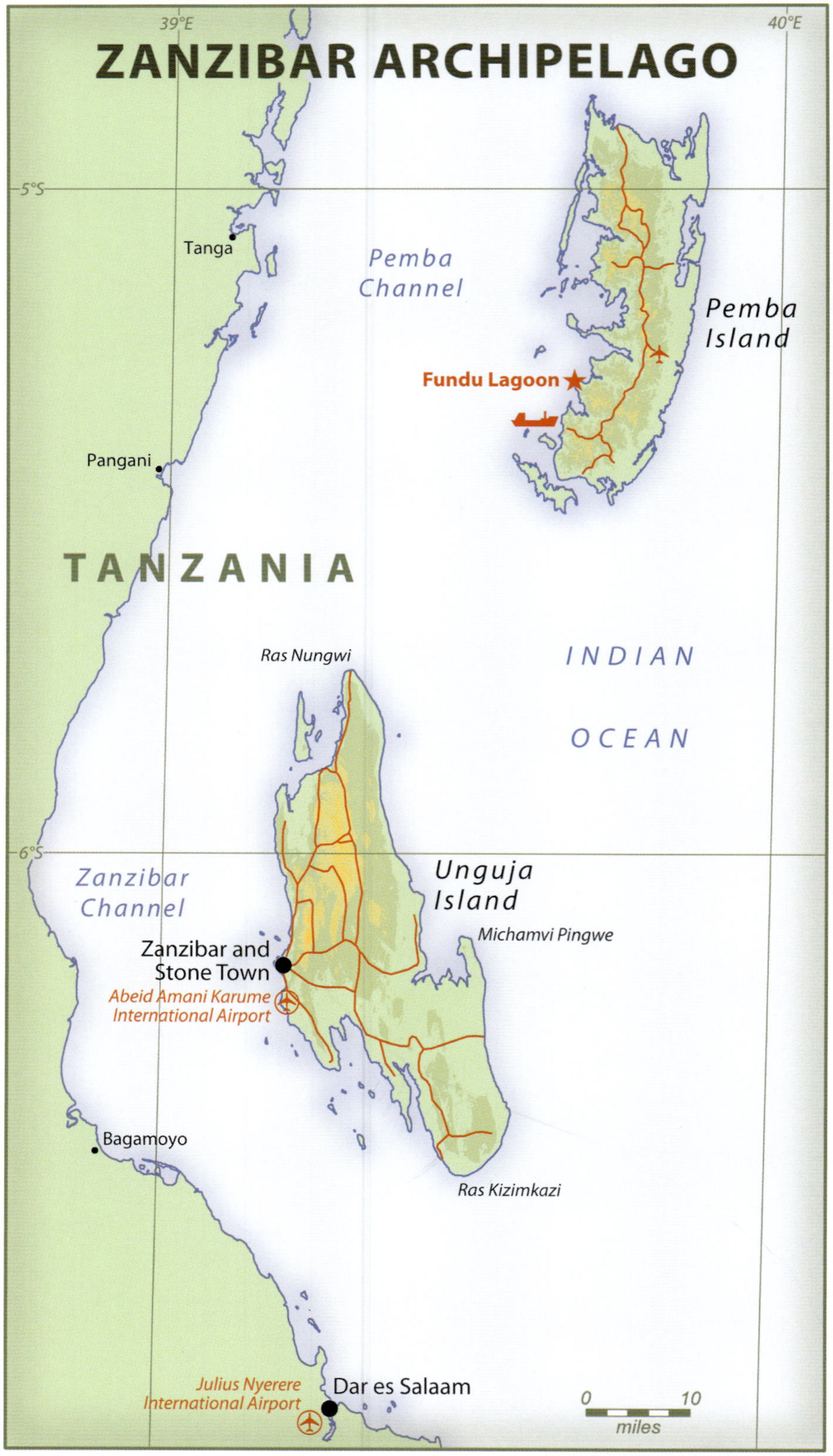
ZANZIBAR ARCHIPELAGO
39°E
40°E
5°S
6°S
Tanga
Pangani
Bagamoyo
Dar es Salaam
Julius Nyerere
International Airport
TANZANIA
Pemba
Channel
Pemba
Island
Fundu Lagoon
Ras Nungwi
INDIAN
OCEAN
Zanzibar
Channel
Unguja
Island
Michamvi Pingwe
Zanzibar and
Stone Town
Abeid Amani Karume
International Airport
Ras Kizimkazi
0
10
miles

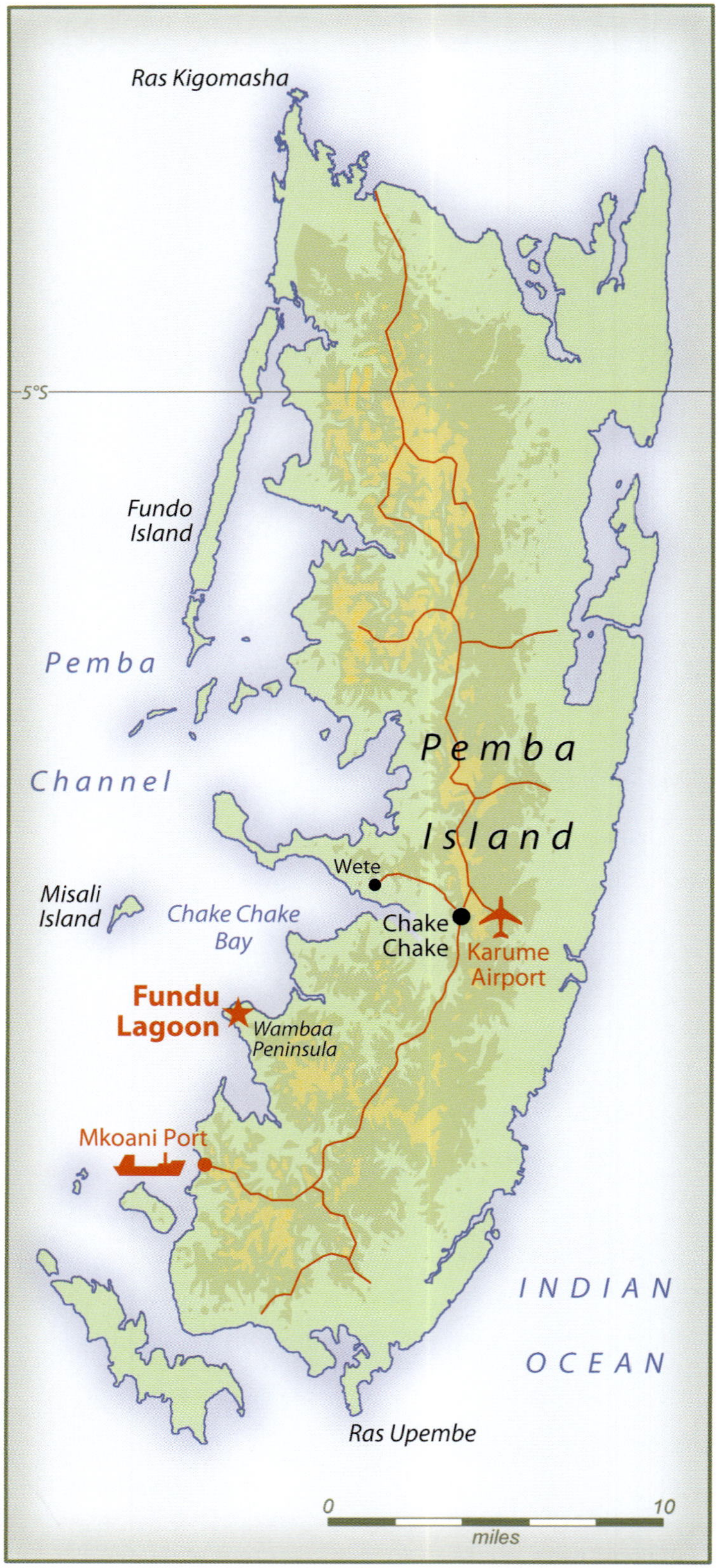
Ras Kigomasha
5°S
Fundo
Island
Pemba
Channel
Pemba
Island
Wete
Misali
Island
Chake Chake
Bay
Chake
Chake
Karume
Airport
Fundu
Lagoon
Wambaa
Peninsula
Mkoani Port
INDIAN
OCEAN
Ras Upembe
0
10
miles

CONTENTS

	Page:
THIS IS FUNDU LAGOON	1
THE VERY BEGINNING	5
FINDING A BEACH	13
BUILDING SANDCASTLES	27
LEARNING THE ROPES	91
THE DARK SIDE	109
THE JOURNEY CONTINUES	113
A BIGGER SPLASH	125
THE FINAL WORD	135

JIM
...navigating with my father's old compass to wherever the wind may take us...

GONZO
Off to Zanzibar...to meet the Zanzibarbarians!

RIZZO
Oh brother! Here they go again!

THE VERY BEGINNING

"That first visit was life-changing. Zanzibar hit me on a deep emotional level. I was knocked out by the place and people. The timing was perfect - I was searching for something... This was where I wanted to be."

Ellis Flyte

www.fundulagoon.com

www.fundulagoon.com

Fundu Lagoon's roots can be firmly traced back to the mid nineties. At that time Brian Henson, of the Jim Henson Company, was directing Muppet Treasure Island. Ellis Flyte, his wife, was an award-winning fashion and costume designer with a successful label, Flyte Ostell. They both needed a break from their hectic trans-Atlantic schedules.

Ellis' growing passion for African art prompted Brian to suggest a Tanzanian safari holiday ending with a few days in Zanzibar, a place Ellis had always wanted to visit. What she found there was, she said, "A magical, mysterious place with a definite air of adventure, both unsettling and intriguing."

At this time Zanzibar's tourist industry was in its infancy. Emerson House Hotel had recently opened in Stone Town on Unguja, the local name for the largest island many visitors call Zanzibar. On that first holiday, Ellis and Brian enjoyed a sunset supper on the rooftop and met the flamboyant owner, Emerson Skeens, for a drink beneath the billowing silk awnings.

"I had no idea at that point that my future would become so entwined with the islands," recalled Ellis. She and Brian spent just three days in Zanzibar before heading home to London, but the magic of the place had made an indelible impression. "I think Ellis fell in love with Zanzibar on that first visit." said Brian. "The people are just so lovely."

Ellis resolved to return, which she did several times on her own in the following couple of years.

In 1997, Ellis decided to take a sabbatical from running her successful business. This new-found time enabled her to make further ad hoc trips. Very soon Zanzibar became Ellis' inspiration, retreat and passion: she had found a new focus. "As a designer I believe you can move into different areas. If you are visually aware, you are affected and inspired by everything around you."

It was around this time that Brian and Ellis amicably separated, although they remain close friends. Brian was to become a vital contributor and advisor to the nascent Zanzibar project.

Today it is easy to see why Ellis is so emotionally attached to these small equatorial islands off the east coast of Africa. During one of her early tours around Unguja, Ellis stayed in Nungwi on the northern coast and was dazzled by the beaches there. Back then Nungwi was little more than a hippy backpacker destination. Ten US dollars bought a simple bed and shared bathroom, bare concrete floors and definitely no creature comforts. Nungwi was also an easy place to meet other travellers; a boon for Ellis travelling on her own in a Muslim society that was conservative and male orientated.

It was the ocean that first attracted Ellis to Zanzibar. "Those early days on far-off beaches were like a dream. I've always loved the sea," she said, "I could rest, re-find myself and try to figure out what I was going to do in Zanzibar." Ellis' ideas began to take shape at this time. "My initial thought was to build a holiday home as an escape from city life." Her local research began with tours around the east coast, viewing dozens of properties, looking at the local architectural vernacular and considering all of the possibilities.

It wasn't until she had returned to the UK that Ellis had the opportunity to think clearly about her proposed plan. She questioned whether it made sense to build a holiday home that would inevitably be underused, overly expensive and contribute little to an island economy that obviously needed help. "It quickly became clear to me that this could become something much more significant," she said. "I wondered if a beach hotel that included a welfare project could help give the local people a chance for a better life." It was an exciting prospect, but how was a single woman going to pull that off? The dream began to unravel.

Ellis' great friend Bryan Reeves, the proprietor of African Escape, a tribal art gallery based in London, had some land in Zanzibar on Unguja island. She agreed to travel out to look at it, and the effect was galvanising. After some excited discussion, it was thought that a small beach hotel was the way forward and Bryan Reeves' east coast plot might possibly be the perfect site for it.

Ellis immediately started thinking about design ideas for a hotel, admitting that her ideas were based more on film than fashion. "I had visions of walking onto a Robinson Crusoe movie set. From the start I was keen that any development should sit unobtrusively in the natural landscape. The shapes, forms and materials should be complementary, and at the same time I wanted to blend international flavours, primarily African, but with harmonious nods to India and the UK too. This concept became the driving force behind the entire project."

Much of Fundu Lagoon's story hinges on fate and nowhere more so than at this crucial point - another chance meeting, this time between Ellis and an old friend Marcus Lewis on a street in Soho, London. After catching up on news, she mentioned her Zanzibar idea. Marcus was immediately interested. He explained that he and his twin brother Alex, after ten years with their building and decorating company, Twin Decs, had also decided it was time to do something new.

Ellis' Zanzibar concept intrigued Marcus. Perhaps this was the opportunity for change that he was looking for, even though Zanzibar was a complete mystery to him. "I didn't know where it was," he later recalled, "it was an atlas job!"

The friends soon realised that their skills were complementary. Ellis' vision and design ethos married well with Marcus' practical building know-how. Rudimentary ideas were hatched, but they still needed a beach. Going into a partnership with Bryan Reeves on the east coast seemed the most realistic option; they had to organise another trip to Zanzibar.

Ellis Flyte   Alex Lewis   Marcus Lewis

FINDING A BEACH

Keen to maintain the momentum, Ellis and Marcus travelled out to Zanzibar a couple of months later, in March 1998.

The initial enthusiasm generated by the project wasn't shared by Marcus' twin brother Alex, and he remained in London looking after their UK business interests. "I see Ellis and Marcus as artists. I'm not an artist - they create things, I'm more the business brains."

Ellis and Marcus' friend Rebecca Osborne, who had offered to help with PR on the budding project, joined them. "I had a call from Ellis who said, 'I'm thinking of buying a beach, will you come with me?' How irresistable was that?!"

Zanzibar's Stone Town had an immediate effect on the newcomers: it seduced them, as it had Ellis on her first visit three years previously.

Over the following few days they hired a Jeep, a decrepit vehicle that spent as much time broken-down off the road as on it, and pottered around the island. Ellis took Marcus and Rebecca north to Nungwi. Marcus took to it immediately: "Ponytails, henna tattoos and fun. I got into the groove and partied. The whole island was such a cool place, I was blown away." Rebecca too was full of enthusiasm: "I couldn't believe the colour of the water, it was like jade and the sand sparkled like ground-up chandeliers."

However, the friends hadn't come to Zanzibar to party. There was a purpose to the trip; it was to be exploratory, they needed to see Bryan Reeves' land.

At that time the road leading from Zanzibar's capital, Stone Town, to the south east coast was a navigable, albeit bumpy, ride along pot-holed compacted earth. Huge plumes of dry, bone-white dust kicked up into the air as they drove to the coastal area of Michamvi Pingwe and turned off onto a sandy track heading to Reeves' beach. Bryan was waiting for them. Just like Ellis, Marcus was beguiled by the long stretches of white sand.

On their return to Stone Town, they began to make serious plans. "I've heard people talk about buying into something like this so many times. They get hypnotised, but most people go home and never do it," said Marcus. Yet for both him and Ellis the timing was perfect.

Back in London they were determined to make it happen and an outline budget for the project was agreed with the other two team members, Alex Lewis and Brian Henson.

It was essential to Marcus that Alex understood the project and shared his enthusiasm, so three months later he joined the next trip out to the islands. Ellis also invited her parents, Tom and Margaret Duncan, who were excited to see what their daughter was up to. Tom, a celebrated architect, had offered to help and began by drawing up a feasibility study for a boutique beach hotel. It seemed the plan was coming together at last.

However, after much deliberation, they all decided this beach wasn't quite right. They also feared that Unguja island was in danger of becoming over-developed, even though tourism was in its infancy in Zanzibar. If this location wasn't right, then what was?

Thomas Hynd Duncan, Ellis and Margaret

Tom, Margaret and Alex left Ellis and Marcus in Zanzibar trying to resurrect the plans for a hotel. They began making tentative enquiries about alternative land through their new and growing network of friends.

During a break in Nungwi, Ellis and Marcus met John Banks, the proprietor of the Fat Fish restaurant and bar. John told them about a remote and undeveloped island to the north of Unguja called Pemba. Ellis and Marcus were intrigued.

Others weren't so impressed. Ellis remembers that most people she spoke to about Pemba were negative. "Don't go there," she was told. "Don't even think about Pemba, there's nothing there." Rather than deter her, the words of warning made Ellis keener to explore the region. There was nothing to lose so they chartered a small plane and flew over the island. From the air Pemba looked utterly untouched. This was an island that needed further investigation.

By their next visit in September, John Banks had made it his business to embed himself in the project and he helped them charter a catamaran named Coelacanth. He was persuasive, full of bluster and convincing bonhomie and was quick to ingratiate himself with these prospective hoteliers. After filling the graceful boat with provisions, they all headed up to Pemba.

"The trip over was really rough," recalled Ellis, "but once we got there I was enchanted." Pemba's lush verdant coastline is thickly vegetated with palms and mangrove. It was the Robinson Crusoe fantasy that Ellis had envisaged. "We went far up the western coast and dropped anchor in a small isolated bay. It was beguiling."

Their first serious foray was onto Fundo Island, a slender elegant stretch of white sand far across the bay from the small town of Wete, some three quarters of the way up Pemba's west coast. A dinghy whisked them over the improbably azure water to shore where, in the exhausting tropical heat, Ellis and Marcus began to pace out the proposed site.

Although an undoubtedly beautiful spot, Fundo Island had its own set of difficulties. There was no obvious source of fresh water and it was home to several fishing villages that Ellis and Marcus did not want to disturb. Realistic talks about logistics and associated problems eventually ruled out that particular splinter of paradise.

For Ellis and Marcus' second trip to Pemba Island in December, a team was assembled: John, skipper Rob, crewmate Emma and chef Hamisi, who were joined by Patrick, a Kenyan foreman, with a view to helping later in the venture.

Their overnight passage aboard Coelacanth was blighted some way north of Unguja island by a sudden, violent storm. Rain lashed down and waves crashed into the boat, this was no ordinary squall. Rob decided that there was only one course of action he could safely take: he'd have to beach Coelacanth and wait for the storm to pass.

Ellis remembers the boat being overbearingly hot and muggy. "All the windows were closed because of the storm, we couldn't breathe, it felt as though we were melting. Even though we were grounded, waves still pummelled the boat."

After a long, frightening night the storm eventually ceased as abruptly as it had begun. Rob opened the doors just as dawn was breaking. The sun hung like a giant red molten ball over a sea as flat as glass.

Everyone went out on deck, relieved to escape the stifling confines of the cabin. Hamisi said, "There's nothing here..." But the moment and place were a revelation to Ellis and Marcus, it was as if fate had taken them there. Ellis turned to Marcus and said, "This is it!"

They weren't to know it yet, but they had landed on the beach of the Wambaa Peninsula. This photogenic finger of land protrudes from the southern end of Pemba's sheltered western shore above the small town of Mkoani. Destiny had brought them to the perfect location for Fundu Lagoon, its name taken from Fundo to the north.

LEFT TO RIGHT:
Naaman, *Chairman Mkoani District*
Marcus Lewis
Bomba, *District Commissioner Mkoani*
David Mwakanjuki, *Police Commissioner Mkoani*
Village Representative
Omar Ali, *Sheha (Village Chief)*

Curious villagers, most of whom weren't familiar with white westerners, came down to the shore to look at the visitors. The chef, Hamisi, acted as translator and soon established that the owner of the land was a Mr Rashid. Mr Rashid and the village chief, or Sheha, came to speak with them.

The Sheha, a wise and kind man, wanted to know if and how their project would benefit his people. Ellis and Marcus assured him that they would employ local villagers during the construction, and also to work in the resort once it was completed. Perhaps most importantly, they promised to help support local welfare from the outset.

Mr Rashid and the Sheha left the new arrivals on the beach and went away to discuss the proposal at length in the village.

Meanwhile, Rob had managed to re-float Coelacanth and Ellis and Marcus clambered back on board. "We hung out on the boat waiting and heard nothing for a couple of days."

Time has a strange habit of stretching in this part of the world and it began to feel as if they might have to wait forever.

On the equator, the sun goes down at 6:30pm pretty much the whole year round. December 13th happened to be Ellis' birthday and the approaching sundown was the signal for Rob to open a bottle to celebrate the special occasion. However, he was stopped suddenly by Patrick. A small dugout canoe was coming across the water containing the Sheha and a couple of other men.

Rob helped the Sheha up the steps. He had never been aboard a boat like Coelacanth before and wanted a tour of the galley, shower and cabins. The experience made him laugh.

Finally he pulled a piece of damp, scrunched-up paper from his pocket. He carefully unravelled it and read in Swahili, "The people of Wambaa accept and welcome you." Hands were shaken and backs slapped. A price for the land would be negotiated the next day. In the meantime, the Sheha and his friends left with a small gift from the boat: Coca-Cola and some duty free cigarettes. It was a birthday Ellis will never forget.

The next day John, with Patrick's translating skills, spent the afternoon under the shade of a coconut palm negotiating with the Sheha to buy the land. It was just one of many palm trees that had to be counted, as Pemban land is measured from tree to tree, prohibiting the cutting down of these essential landmarks. The number of trees would determine the price to be paid.

The adventure was about to move into a new phase.

Back on board Coelacanth, Ellis and Marcus immediately began to sketch out ideas for the new site. Crew mate Emma hesitantly offered to help. "I was out of my depth and nervous, I didn't know Ellis or Marcus well, but I remember Ellis talking about her dad's plans and I said that perhaps I could help…"

It transpired that Emma was on a gap year from an architectural course in South Africa. Ellis wanted to know what her plans were. Perhaps she was the missing piece of the jigsaw.

"That Emma was on the boat felt like another twist of fate," said Ellis. "I sensed she had great energy and from her drawings, terrific talent as an architect." It would be Emma's job to start work on a general plan for the hotel.

A time frame of nine months was hastily put together. The team would return to Zanzibar in the New Year and start construction as soon as possible. Budget constraints meant the hotel would have to open within a year.

BUILDING SANDCASTLES

The enormity of the task ahead became apparent during the festive season. With the general outline and architectural sketches of the hotel agreed, and the budget in place, it was time for the teams to set to work.

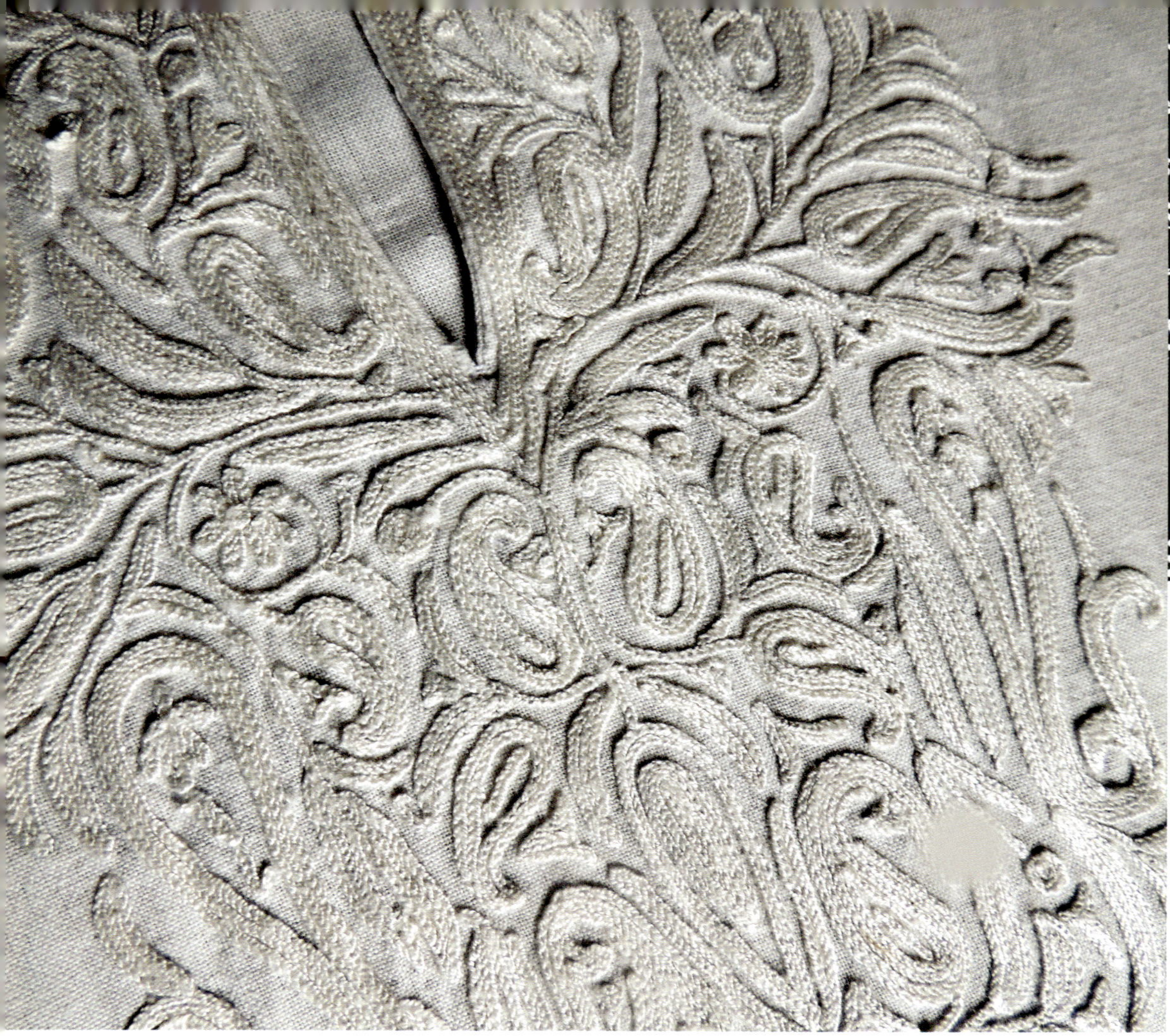

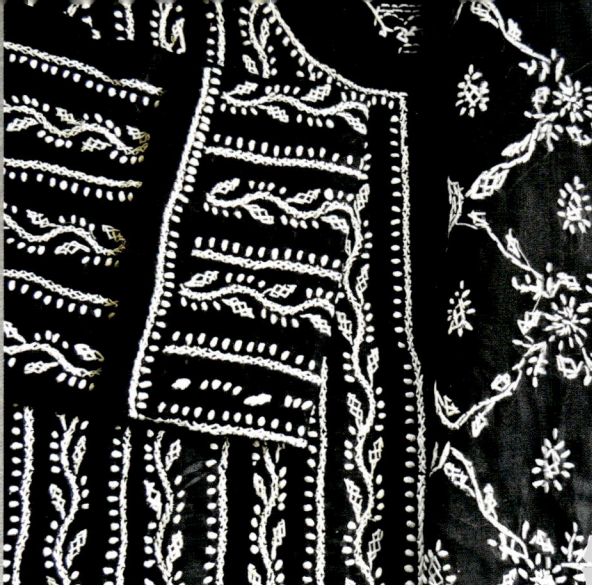

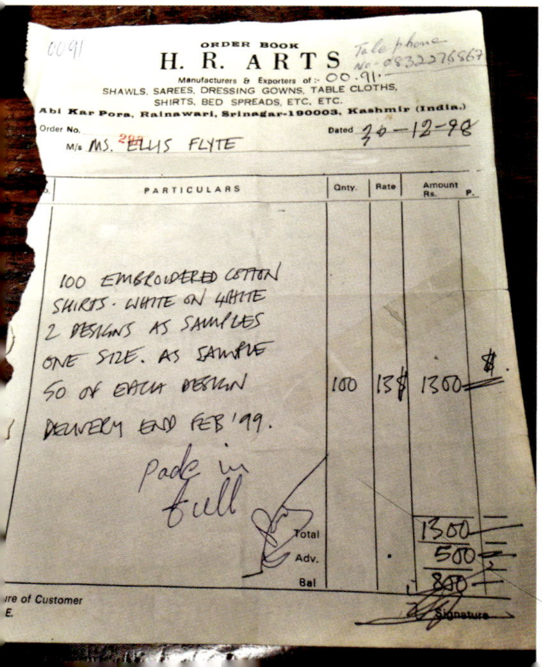
00 91

ORDER BOOK

H. R. ARTS Tele phone No- 08322276867

Manufacturers & Exporters of :- 00.91.
SHAWLS, SAREES, DRESSING GOWNS, TABLE CLOTHS,
SHIRTS, BED SPREADS, ETC. ETC.

Abi Kar Pora, Rainawari, Srinagar-190003, Kashmir (India.)

Order No. 20- Dated 30-12-98

M/s MS. ELLIS FLYTE

PARTICULARS	Qnty.	Rate	Amount Rs.	P.
100 EMBROIDERED COTTON SHIRTS. WHITE ON WHITE 2 DESIGNS AS SAMPLES ONE SIZE. AS SAMPLE 50 OF EACH DESIGN DELIVERY END FEB '99.	100	13$	1300	$
Paid in full				
Total			1300	
Adv.			500	
Bal			800	

ure of Customer
E.

Signature

Just days after the land purchase had been agreed, and now finally able to realise her vision, Ellis made a prearranged journey to India, seeking more inspiration for Fundu Lagoon's distinctive look. Here she sourced elaborately embroidered Kashmiri shirts, the perfect look for waiting staff, and beautiful cut-work blankets for the rooms.

This initial expedition was the first of many exploratory trips that helped crystallise the cultural fusion Ellis was seeking. Now she needed to tackle the huge logistical problems and start making her creative ideas a reality.

By the end of January, back in London, Ellis began the vast task of equipping the hotel with basics. The procurement process was colossal; everything from plates, glassware and cutlery, through to towels, toilets and basins, had to be sourced and purchased, checked, invoiced, packed and itemised ready for dispatch by container ship to Pemba.

The huge daily deliveries that arrived at Ellis' home made it look like a depot. Most of the buying was UK based, because during the nineties the quality of goods and style options were not available in Tanzania.

Abdi Haji Usi   Marcus Lewis   Abas Juma   Patrick Ngundi

Ellis Flyte

Marcus returned to Zanzibar at the end of January 1999, where it was planned that Emma would initially stay for two or three weeks to help map out the newly acquired site. She set up a drawing board on the veranda at John Banks' house in Nungwi and began working on the layout in earnest, discussing concepts with Marcus and Ellis, who had arrived to finalise the plans. Ellis then submitted the drawings to the government office in Stone Town before heading back to London to report on progress to Brian.

By the end of February, they returned to Wambaa with Patrick, Abdi (a Zanzibari foreman) and Abas (a Zanzibari store-man), to start building with the new plans. They were to sail to Pemba on a concrete boat called Citra that John had sourced. Its two cabins were to double as temporary accommodation for Marcus and Emma, not that they thought they'd be on it for long. All aboard were relieved to finally drop anchor because the crossing was tough and Citra, they discovered, was barely seaworthy.

As they disembarked, they were welcomed by several villagers and led to a small cassava plantation behind the mangroves where the Sheha awaited them. Everyone was interested in the programme of works, but Emma remembered that the plan they had been handed by John was just a scrawled list of three points:

1. Dig a well
2. Build a site office
3. Build a storeroom

They began with point one, and asked the villagers, with Patrick acting as translator, where to dig the well, making the assumption that they would have local expertise. Excited conversation pirouetted among the interested bystanders before finally coming to a definitive answer: nobody knew. So who had dug their village well? It had been a gift from the United Nations.

Marcus made his first executive decision - they would dig where they stood. Four village men were hired on the spot and excavation got underway in the sticky heat. A ragged sail from an ngalawa, a local dug-out canoe, was thrown up for shade. After two days of digging by hand with picks and shovels and two cave-ins, at seven metres depth they hit water. It was fresh and would supply the entire site for the following year.

What neither Marcus nor Emma knew then was that the discovery of fresh water had been a fluke. Much later it would take professional drillers many attempts before they found water. Fate had dealt a helping hand once more.

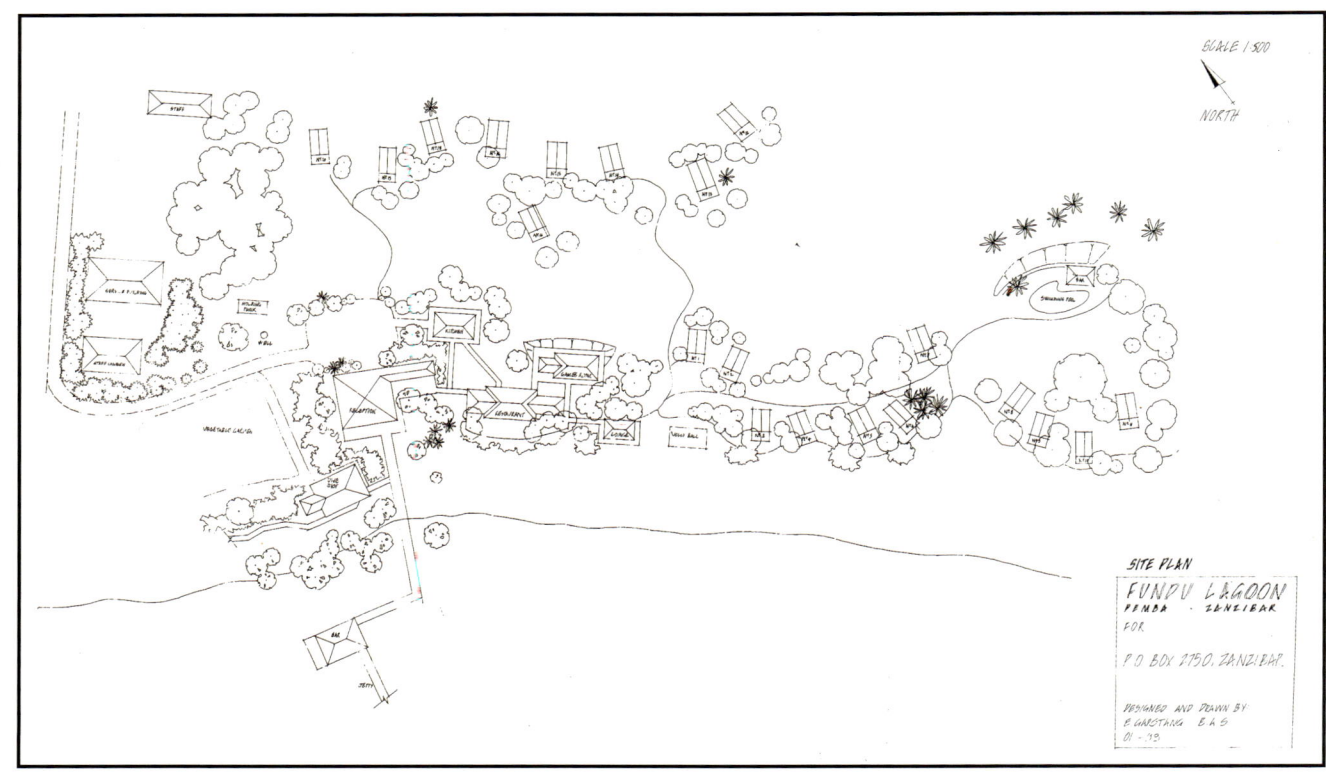

Emma Garstang

Now they were on site, it became evident to Emma that her initial drawings would need serious revision, in fact she would have to start again from scratch. She would also have to rebuild her relationship with the villagers. Soon after arriving, she had made a serious cultural faux pas by walking onto the beach in a T-shirt and shorts; unwittingly she'd caused outrage in the traditionally conservative Muslim community. "It put me in a very bad light in the beginning, I was blanked by people."

Emma quickly adopted an appropriate working uniform of a kanga over her shorts and a button-up long-sleeved cotton shirt. Even so, it took some time before the local women forgave her sartorial error.

With the well now in operation, work could begin on the store and site office; simple wooden frames on concrete floors with makuti thatch roofs made from dried palm leaves, a local vernacular that would become an integral part of the hotel design.

Momentum on the site began to build quickly. Patrick, Abdi and Abas went into the local villages to ask for

twenty extra men to come for work the following day.

Early next morning two hundred men waited expectantly for work. Alarmed, Marcus told Patrick to choose those who were needed. He refused point blank. Marcus had to make the choice. "I could pick the men because I didn't know them or the local politics. I was picking blind in effect with no favouritism." Sending a hundred and eighty men home without work that day was an intimidating experience.

Now the core group of twenty had been established, there was a lengthy discussion about wages, which was eventually unanimously agreed with the help of the Sheha. Bringing a cash economy into the area needed to be handled with great sensitivity as most villagers lived by either subsistence farming or fishing. To suddenly start employing a minority of people and paying them way over the neighbourhood odds would upset the local economy and create localised inflation. With the Sheha's wise advice, a compromise was reached. It felt as if the balance was about right.

Even though the logistics of building on Wambaa had been considered, they had been woefully underestimated. Now that the store and office were under construction another important building needed to go up. A mosque was quickly erected, but in haste it had been constructed facing the wrong direction! It had to be reorientated to face Mecca. A kitchen was also needed to provide food for everyone on site. Local women or 'mamas' ran the kitchen like generals, producing huge quantities of food at meal times.

Marcus and Emma had seen how some 'mzungus', the Swahili word for white people, ate lavishly in Unguja, while expecting workers to eat basics. From the beginning on the construction site the food was to be exactly the same for everyone. It was a leveller. There were no privileges, which meant drinking tea at breakfast that had the viscosity of honey. Emma tried asking the mamas to make it without sugar. She was given short logical Pemban shrift; without sugar, "then it not chai!"

Each day was the same. Before work started at 7.30am there was a breakfast of sweetened noodles and bread. Rice and beans were served for lunch and dinner, except on Fridays when goat pilau was on the menu, and on Tuesdays fish might be dished up.

Apart from the mountains of food required to fill an ever increasing number of stomachs, the build developed its own appetite and began to consume vast volumes of materials. Yet again Patrick, Abdi and Abas were instrumental in galvanising the project by finding reliable local sources of sand, coral rock, timber and makuti.

Boats proved to be even more essential to the build than originally envisaged. Because there was no road infrastructure on Pemba, absolutely everything was brought directly to the beach at the site on board ngalawas - even the sand, which was excavated inland as beach sand was too salty and would destroy the concrete mix. Construction became beholden to the tide: there was no jetty at this time, so deliveries could only be made at high water.

The initial trickle of ngalawas soon became a tsunami. When jahazis, majestic over-sized dhows that look like billowing Spanish galleons, arrived containing cargoes of 2,000 bags of cement at a time, the entire workforce would come down to the beach to help unload.

Makuti thatch for roofs is traditionally plaited by women, but as there were not enough people locally to meet demand, runners were sent around the island to commission it from other communities. At one point it seemed as if the whole of Pemba was making thatch for Fundu Lagoon. This was gathered into vast

piles on the quayside in Mkoani, loaded onto jahazis and sailed to site.

Coral rock arrived on ngalawas and was thrown over the side at high tide to be collected at low tide and stacked into piles on the beach.

The large poles for the wooden frames of all the buildings were floated in behind the boats. It took four men to carry each pole up from the beach. The site required 4,500 of these.

Communication between the site and Unguja island, or further afield, was limited to passing letters by couriers on local ferries. A simple message would take at least twenty four hours to be answered.

Nowhere on Pemba had seen a building project on this scale before - it was epic. The construction methods employed in this hugely complicated scheme were frankly ancient. The Omani sultans would have recognised many of the same techniques several centuries earlier.

It wasn't just the antiquated building methods that slowed progress. The unrelenting heat regularly topped 35 degrees Celsius, and the start of the build had coincided with the beginning of the holy month of Ramadan. All the workers on site were observant and took neither food nor water during daylight hours. Work finished by 2pm each day because no-one had the energy to carry on.

Meanwhile John had established deep roots within the Fundu organisation. He had created a monopoly on sourcing the supplies from Unguja and mainland Tanzania. He also supplied some of the workforce; in other words he'd made himself central to the operation. His sporadic visits to site were always brief and the idea that he would run the construction somehow never materialised.

"Strangely he gave us the confidence to carry on," said Emma, "because we

always thought that he'd take over and make everything alright." However she noticed a disconnection between what John had in his head and what Ellis and Marcus had in theirs. On one occasion he sent plastic shower trays up to the site - they were completely out of keeping with the design ethos. Emma began to wonder if they were under the misguided impression that John knew what he was doing.

The hot, uncomfortable, cramped and grubby accommodation on Citra had become a permanent fixture for Marcus and Emma. During the spring tides everything was permanently wet. Sanitation was rudimentary. There was no toilet on board, only a bucket. "I found it really awkward," Emma remembered, "but we developed a brother/sister relationship and coped." They bathed on site in a rudimentary shower made from a jerrycan propped up behind a screen.

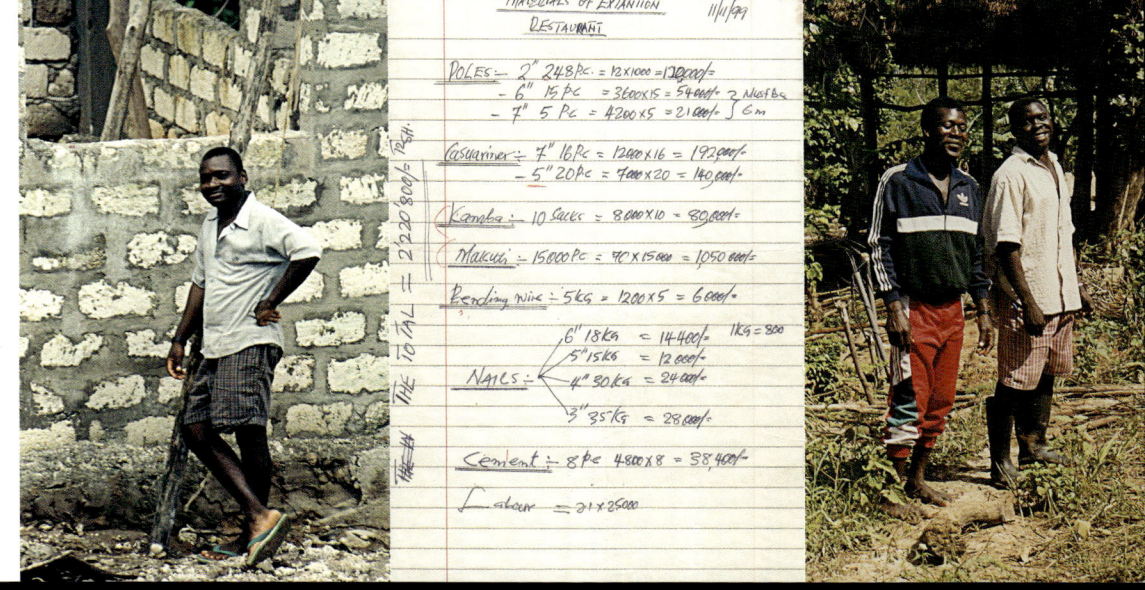

Impetus on the build had to be maintained; positions of significant buildings were paced out and ditches and trenches dug for cables and infrastructure. After work had been underway for about a month the site resembled a battleground. It was at this point, in March, that Alex made his first visit to Pemba with Ellis.

"When I stepped off the boat I knew instantly this was it, I didn't question the site for a second. There was very little to see, no jetty, just a clearing, an office and a well. That was it… and a lot of ditches, ditches and mud everywhere!"

Ellis and Alex's visit was important for another reason. The site was in desperate need of funds. Banking facilities were basic in Dar es Salaam, crude in Stone Town and non-existent on Pemba. The only surefire way of getting money to where it was needed back then was to carry it. Ellis and Alex both arrived on site with cash discreetly hidden on their person.

It began to look as if their budgets had been underestimated. Other than makuti, coral rock and sand, Pemba had nothing that could be bought easily. Everything else had to be imported, which added to the costs significantly. Setting up an office in Stone Town became paramount so that items bought further afield could be collated and shipped to site through it.

In Stone Town other problems also awaited Ellis and Marcus. They discovered that the rights to the plot on Wambaa were not what they understood them to be. It transpired that they had in fact bought only the trees on the site and not the actual land. The deal they had naively struck with the Sheha was compensation for the palms, nothing else. When they went to submit the architect's drawings, they discovered that they would have to register the land and pay for a land lease from the Zanzibar Revolutionary Government to establish the right to build on Pemba.

At this point in the build, Emma expected to leave. However, Marcus and Ellis asked her to stay on and continue to coordinate essential works on site and help with the design and spec for the furniture.

Ellis also needed to further develop her idea of how the furnishings should look. She wanted to reference the easy-going luxury of a safari camp while embracing comfort and island chic. This was no easy task, especially as the quantities involved were astounding; hundreds of chairs, dozens of beds, wardrobes, tables, blinds, sofas and scores of sun-beds needed to be acquired, but from where?

With the Wambaa carpentry workshop stretched to capacity, some furniture would have to be outsourced to other workshops around Pemba, and even as far as Unguja. This added stress and logistical complications with coordinating and supervising distant workforces and the quality of the finished pieces.

When the furniture was finally varnished and ready to collect, the word went out to find any kind of vehicle large enough to provide transportation to the waiting boats at Mkoani harbour. Vehicles of all shapes and sizes appeared, including dala dala buses normally used to carry passengers.

In the spring Ellis planned a trip to Morocco in search of lamps and other furnishings. On this journey she was joined by boyfriend Neil Pascoe, who was fascinated by the African project and keen to get involved. They travelled to Marrakech together.

After exploring local markets for days, goat skin and henna lamps caught Ellis' eye. She bought dozens of them, as well as metal lanterns to place around the hotel. Shipping them directly from Morocco to Zanzibar proved too difficult so they went on a circuitous journey via London. Unfortunately, the goat skin lamps lasted barely three months in Fundu; they went mouldy in the humidity. Ever resourceful and imaginative, the skin was stripped off them and coconut string was wound around the metal frames instead. They looked good and are still in use today.

Ellis was also keen to source natural soaps and bath products from the plentiful supply in Zanzibar, but nothing there was quite right. Back in London Alex's wife, Camilla, introduced her friend Richard Howard to Ellis. He had a small business called Arcania Apothecary, also responsible for the Cow Shed brand.

Richard came out to Fundu as an early guest and was mesmerised by the wonderful local flora. He returned to the UK and developed a range of products specifically for Fundu Lagoon: soap, shampoo, conditioner, after-sun and massage oils designed around plants he found there. As a spa proprietor himself, Richard also assisted Ellis in setting up the resort's own treatment rooms.

There were other items for Ellis to consider too. Dozens of beautiful designer linen dressing gowns were manufactured in the UK, for both the rooms and the proposed gift shop.

For the dive centre, Ellis' friend James Abbott came up with the name Dive 710, reflecting that 7/10ths of the Earth's surface is water, and designed the logos for the clothing. The original products also had to be manufactured in London and shipped out.

Thousands of metres of fabric, including cottons and shower curtain fabric, were sourced and earmarked for export to Zanzibar ready to be made up into soft furnishings and staff uniforms.

Ellis was travelling constantly throughout this period. In June she returned to Zanzibar on another visit; this would be Neil's first trip to Wambaa. She delivered another tranche of cash to the site before returning to Dar es Salaam with Neil to seek out local artisans.

They headed to Mwenge, a market outside Dar es Salaam, unfrequented at that time by tourists, but where traders brought artifacts to sell from all over Tanzania. Masks, sculptures, jewellery, hand-crafted fabrics and beautiful African artifacts were laid out on the dusty ground.

"I was absolutely delighted and astounded by the different faces of tribal Tanzania - serious masks mostly, very beautiful," recalled Ellis.

They found fabrics that would add vivid colour to walls and other areas around the hotel.

Neil had become an important part of the team. "Culturally it's very difficult for a single white woman travelling in these destinations," said Ellis. "I had to negotiate deals through Neil with many of the tradespeople we did business with, not just in Zanzibar, but all over the world. He also arranged the packing and shipping of furniture, fridges, cookers and uniforms into boxes, containers and boats."

Neil recalls, "It was the biggest thing I had known - Fundu Lagoon changed my life. Travelling and meeting new people showed me a whole different world."

The hotel still needed suitable seating for the restaurant and lounge areas. With the exception of safari chairs, nothing locally available was satisfactory. Once again it became apparent that trips further afield were needed.

Neil's input was nowhere more valuable than on the first trip to Malawi in search of the vast quantities of British colonial-style wicker furniture needed for the resort.

A contact in Zanzibar had told Ellis about the furniture makers of Salima, a small township in central Malawi. They flew into the capital Lilongwe, hired a car and driver and set off. It was to be no ordinary road trip.

After driving for several hours they arrived in Salima at nightfall. To Ellis' dismay there appeared to be no furniture artisans. They bedded down in a local hotel for the night, feeling disappointed.

The next morning brought some relief. The furniture makers had not been visible because they worked in shaded areas hidden away from the roadsides. The craftsmen had primitive facilities. Sticks propped up ragged tarpaulins, simple tables held a few meagre tools, but the wicker and carved furniture they produced was beautiful.

Ellis had with her Polaroid pictures of the designs that she wanted them to follow and these became central to the simple contracts. Neil, after discreetly discussing tactics with Ellis, sat down with the craftsmen to negotiate prices and place the orders. Half of the money would be paid up front, the balance on completion.

Neil remembers the journey back to Lilongwe vividly. "Our drive was unlike anything I'd experienced before. At one point we slowed down as we met men armed with spears. They came out of the long grass wearing masks, it was daunting. I didn't know how to act, it wasn't a good time to stop and find out!"

Back on Pemba, the workforce had spiralled up from the core group of twenty to around a hundred and fifty. Not only had employee costs increased, but workers from the villages also wanted breakfast and lunch included, and supper had to be provided for the twenty or so tradesmen who lived on site.

Around one third of the workforce were local women who were responsible for most of the hard labour. They moved huge coral rocks balanced on their heads to wherever they were needed throughout the site – the same rock would take two men to carry by hand. Yet the men insisted they be paid twice as much as the women.

Work for both men and women was arduous and Emma decided that as both sexes were working equally hard, pay parity was only fair. It was proposed the women's wage be doubled. A meeting was called but the idea was not received well. The suggestion that they be paid the same as men outraged some of the crowd and the debate became heated and threatened to escalate. After much deliberation the problem was resolved on the advice of the Sheha, who determined women would receive pay parity and the build would continue.

Emma and Marcus continued to peg out positions for the restaurant and reception area, continually making adjustments as they went along. The communication difficulties with the Stone Town operation and further afield were now becoming a significant problem and a serious threat to progress. After six weeks of ferrying messages between the islands, a satellite phone was brought out to Pemba by Ellis. There was no mobile phone connection at that time - the sat-phone, a big clunky object with an accompanying satellite dish, represented the very latest in mobile technology.

Now it was possible to call through with orders and speed up the acquisition process. A small generator soon followed; the site had its own power supply at long last.

The second stage of building, the areas back-of-house, began to kick in. These included the hotel storerooms, kitchen, laundry and all the other areas of operation that go on unseen by guests. Colossal amounts of earth were dug out of the hill to level the ground for the kitchens. A local Zebu bull and cart trundled to and fro moving soil around the site, creating the foundations and opportunity to start work on the bungalows.

Despite the oppressive heat, steady progress seemed assured, but Zanzibar has its seasons too, most notably the rainy season. Enormous deluges beat down on Wambaa, filling freshly dug trenches with topsoil or washing away newly excavated foundations. Torrential tropical storms raged relentlessly, making work on the site, now drowning in gluey mud, all but impossible. Illness began to affect the workforce.

Marcus and Emma were unanimous in identifying this period as the most trying and undoubtedly the lowest point during the build. But even though the weather made working conditions nearly intolerable, they never gave up or felt defeated.

Emma and Steven

The first big roof to be built was for the reception area. Emma designed it with Steven Kaingu, a Kenyan contractor who specialised in makuti construction. Steven's knowledge was vital, tweaking the pitch of the roof to withstand regional weather conditions. "Steven had a real instinct for engineering and we created a lovely organic shape between us," Emma recalls.

With a task force of forty men assigned to the roofs, the first job was to hoist a massive A-frame into place by hand. The skeleton of the towering twenty five metre roof space above the reception area resembled a beautiful and intricate wooden spider's web. The men worked without scaffolding and had to be meticulously sure-footed as the slightest slip would have been catastrophic. Fortunately there were no accidents and the roof was ready to be thatched in makuti within a week.

The next project was to start work on the tented bungalows. They were designed with wide open fronts to allow light to flood in and create a sense of being among the treetops. Sourcing the safari-style tents proved difficult. A sample had been ordered in March which did not arrive until June. It was disappointing, as a lot of the detail was incorrect and thread colours seemed to have been chosen at random. The zips and mosquito net windows were substandard as well. The supplier had to remake them, and Ellis and Neil needed to find time to fly into Dar es Salaam to check each completed tent before it was shipped to Fundu.

Room 17 (out of a total of 20) was the first room to be completed, consisting of a platform and tent; it was a significant physical and psychological turning point. Marcus and Emma could move from the cramped, damp confines of Citra into the comparative luxury of a bungalow. No more buckets! After months of making do, they now had running water, a shower and a flushing toilet. Much excitement was generated by the installation of the first hot shower, with the locals laughing at its "hot rain". The project was feeling real. To this day Fundu remains the only tented beach "safari" experience in Tanzania.

Marcus and Emma felt starved of news, so the arrival of any site visitor generated great excitement. "I must have heard Marcus' stories five hundred times but what else was there to do except talk after finishing work?" asked Emma. "Although I read a lot of books, absolutely anything, whatever people left behind!"

The arrival of a visitor on site also brought a welcome change to the normal menu of rice and beans. As a treat, chicken would be cooked. The catching of the chicken became something of a ritual, the scrawny birds doing their athletic best to elude half a dozen men shouting and running after them brandishing kitchen knives.

After the reception roof was put up, the floorboards went down. The kitchens were also progressing well. Now thoughts turned towards building a jetty. Emma designed a structure that reached a hundred metres out into the ocean, but Abdi came up with a novel idea to aid its development. He put poles into concrete-filled buckets, positioned them upright in the sea and moved them around during the following month. This way they could measure the jetty in relationship to the changing tides, rather than having to build the structure on guesswork alone.

The initial hundred metres got longer and longer depending on how far out the tide went. Eventually the final figure was settled - the jetty would be two hundred and thirty metres from end to end. It took six months to build.

The building of Fundu Lagoon involved a huge cast of characters with many different skills. Roofers, painters, mechanics, tailors and wrappers – people responsible for winding handmade twine around the wooden posts. The new team also included a young deaf and dumb orphan from the village who would later become a staff member and skilled mason.

Sometimes cultural norms made working relationships more complicated. Although Emma had been forgiven for her original clothing gaffe, it was still difficult for her to issue instructions on site as a female. She took to giving directions through Patrick, Abdi or Abas, eventually earning the affectionate badge of honour from the workforce of "mama fundi", or craftswoman.

Each morning when work started, Patrick would take a roll call. On pay day the entire workforce would come down to the storeroom and sit patiently in the shade, waiting while bags of Tanzanian shillings were carefully counted out and distributed – wages that were usually signed for with a thumb print.

Back in London, Ellis and Neil frantically carried on buying and packing goods. Everything that had been bought for Fundu during the previous months needed to be shipped. Incredibly this included four yellow speedboats to be used for transfers to the hotel and for diving expeditions. John Banks, on a brief visit to the UK, met with Alex and travelled to Portsmouth where they tested several models, buying two larger and two smaller unsinkable boats of the type once used by the SAS.

These speedboats were packed into a massive container alongside the enormous collection of items amassed by Ellis, including her trusty industrial sewing machine. There was a deadline: the container needed to be shipped by the start of August if it were to arrive in Zanzibar in time for the hotel's soft opening at the end of October. Overseeing the final stages of this process was exhausting, but the job was completed with a day to spare.

A week later, Ellis and Neil flew back to Malawi to pay the balance on the first wicker furniture order. After an arduous trip, they arrived in Salima during torrential rains to discover that nothing was ready. All the furniture still needed to be varnished, but there was none available in the small town. Ellis and Neil had to head back to Lilongwe to source and buy varnish in an effort to salvage the situation.

On the long, hot return journey, Ellis and Neil pulled in for food at the roadside. "We only had eggs and corn to eat," said Neil. "I needed a meat fix from the local barbecue. I thought I was buying small kebabs but I was amazed to see they were field mice!" Nothing was wasted - their driver happily ate the lot.

While in the capital looking for varnish, Ellis also found more unusual tribal carvings and masks which she would send to Zanzibar with the furniture – if it was ever finished. They eventually returned to Salima with the barrel of varnish, but with the hotel opening in less than three months and much still to do, time was running out.

After overseeing the completion of the first furniture batch, and securing a place for it to be stored in a local hotel, Ellis placed the final order and left with Neil once more for a site visit to Pemba.

A month later, in the middle of September, they returned to Salima one last time. To Ellis' relief the furniture order was complete; the craftsmen had worked around the clock to finish the job on time. As a small token of thanks, Ellis and Neil gave the community a bonus and in return the grateful villagers threw a party in their honour.

The huge order of furniture was loaded onto a truck, but before it could leave, the driver insisted that it be hidden with bags of rice to deflect unscrupulous interest on the immense journey by road across Malawi and Tanzania. Once at the coast, it would be transferred to a jahazi and sail the vast distance across the Pemba Channel to Wambaa, weather permitting.

The flurry of activity and excitement became palpable as the build moved into the final phase. Alex and his friends Andy and Lindsay had come out to help with the last push. "We were running teams doing whatever jobs Marcus and Emma handed out," said Alex. "Snagging was done on a massive scale. I was in charge of rooms and I couldn't get distracted, the finish had to be just right. It all suddenly went very fast."

Ellis and Neil were both struggling with exhaustion after their relentless journeying, but there was no opportunity to rest. They too flew back to Zanzibar and headed to Pemba to help complete the project on time.

The enormous container shipment of speedboats, a safe, a Rolls Royce generator, ovens and industrial hobs, freezers, all the china, cutlery and glassware arrived on Wambaa's remote shore. If the size of the shipment was epic by most standards, it was totally off the scale by Pemban measures.

The ship was beached by the mangroves, just past the reception area, and a temporary road was constructed through to it. Dozens of men carefully manoeuvred the heavy cargo off the boat by hand and safely onto dry land.

Ellis had a tailoring shop to set up and run. All the soft furnishings for the hotel needed to be sewn: from mosquito nets, bed sheets, curtains and cushion covers to chefs'

hats, aprons and uniforms. Her old industrial sewing machine was unpacked and set up in one of the back-of-house workshops. "Word went out that I needed more help. Half-a-dozen men showed up carrying old fashioned treadle Singer sewing machines on their heads, including Daniel, who became my head tailor."

Ellis adopted a uniform of trousers, long sleeved shirt and covered head. As a woman, she found it essential to earn respect by dressing with regard to local customs. Ellis explained what was needed by sign language and demonstration. The new workforce was exceptional. She had been accepted and was even allowed to take off her headscarf. Daniel and his son Zaburi still work at Fundu today.

Local law requires that employees are supplied with footwear. "We were so naive, most of these poor villagers had never worn shoes before. We tried hard to fit their feet correctly, but they mostly couldn't walk in the new shoes and resorted to flip flops."

Local craftswomen were working hard too. They began weaving bags, mats, sun hats and lamp shades for the hotel rooms and gift shop. Some of the village children spent afternoons on the beach collecting piles of seed pods that were strung together to make over-sized bead curtains.

Although the container from London had arrived, there was still no sign of the jahazi ferrying the wicker furniture order from Malawi. Ellis remembers looking anxiously out to sea for its arrival. "I thought the furniture had been lost, all of it sunk to the bottom of the sea!"

It eventually arrived in the nick of time, and everyone on site ran down to the beach to help unload, walking through the water carrying chairs, tables and sofas on their heads before the sun went down.

With the tailoring shop well established, it was time for Ellis and Neil to make yet another trip. They returned to Morocco at the start of October in search of more decorative items. There was a window of just eight days to locate the last pieces of the jigsaw before the hotel finally opened its doors for the first time to a group of friends for its soft opening, an engagement which they both absolutely had to attend.

Now that the site had filled with others, Emma found herself reeling with mixed emotions. "All of a sudden my bubble burst, I felt threatened; almost like I'd been robbed."

Her work over, a small party was held for Emma, who finally wrapped up and left one week before the guests arrived.

Despite the belief and use of magic being prevalent throughout Africa, it is especially important on the islands of the Zanzibar archipelago and particularly on Pemba. The richness and diversity of these beliefs is intrinsic to the identity of the island. Pemba's djinn are a remarkably potent force and witch doctors have a lot of power. Their curse can have devastating effects on believers and their blessings can be hugely positive.

News of the potential employment Fundu Lagoon offered spread around the region quickly by word of mouth. Prospective staff from Unguja and the mainland were initially hesitant because of Pemba's tradition as the most important location for voodoo and witch doctors in all of East Africa.

Kessy, one such potential employee from Tanzania, had heard stories of Pemba's djinn and was told that there were, "A lot of witches on Pemba, you have to be very careful!"

Others had also been warned about these unsettling spirits. Yet however likely encounters with the supernatural seemed to be, it didn't discourage dozens of new recruits from arriving.

For some, like Lizzie, there were other obstacles. Lizzie was also terrified of water. The ferry journey to Pemba and connection across the water to Wambaa were a huge ordeal. "I wanted to go home, but it was too late; I was on the ferry. I stayed with my head in my hands the whole trip. When we arrived they asked me to get off the boat into water, as the jetty was not ready. I cried like a baby until I was carried off on someone's shoulders." Both Kessy and Lizzie have built careers at Fundu Lagoon.

Over the years Fundu Lagoon has gone through a series of cleansing rituals performed by local witch doctors to appease the djinn. These ceremonies include hypnotic drumming, the offering of a chicken, goat or bull and trance-like dancing by the villagers.

The local witch doctor's involvement in the genesis of Fundu has reassured villagers that the djinn are happy that the hotel has been established.

The first group of staff came to Pemba on board the ferry Sepideh from Stone Town and were transferred to Wambaa on Fundu's dhow Mama Casa. But it wasn't just the jetty that was unfinished; there were no staff quarters either so the newcomers had to sleep in the guest rooms to begin with. Instead of taking up positions as waiters and storemen, bar staff or cleaners, everyone helped with finishing the hotel.

Sawdust was still being swept out of reception and building detritus cleared from around the site as two boats full of people drew in towards the jetty. Fundu Lagoon's very first guests had arrived. Forty friends, family and contributors were about to become guinea pigs for the next seven days to test the place out.

Ellis had decided to stage a soft opening to road test the resort. It would be an opportunity to assess how the restaurant and bars operated and how housekeeping fitted in around visitors. It would also test the Dive Centre, front-of-house, reception and accounts, and put the transfer arrangements through their paces. Every aspect of Fundu Lagoon would be scrutinised and analysed. Who better to test the hotel's services than family and friends of Ellis and Neil, Marcus and Alex?

Invitations had been sent out earlier in the summer and the lucky recipients were asked to stay for seven nights. Unsurprisingly, the offer was over-subscribed. Everyone wanted to come to Fundu Lagoon to see for themselves the wonderful hotel their friends had created on this exotic-sounding island.

Travelling from Karume airport to the port at Mkoani was torturously slow at the end of the nineties. The roads were unmade red mud baths pitted with huge potholes. Curious villagers came out to watch the small cavalcade of tourists pass by and dozens of shouting children ran alongside.

The heady scent of clove harvests drying in the sun and the sight of exotic tropical fruits growing along the roadside added to the magical adventure. It was difficult to tell who was more excited, the passengers or onlookers.

On the 21st October 1999, the new hoteliers stood on the jetty ready to welcome the excited holiday-makers. Jules Turner, an architect friend, put it succinctly, "None of us on the boat knew what to expect. After the long journey to Mkoani and the boat crossing, we were still none the wiser because the hotel is all but invisible. But when we arrived and Ellis and the twins standing on the jetty came into view, we all started clapping; it was all so very English."

Behind the scenes at Fundu, panic reigned. Not only were the staff still frantically cleaning, but the water supply had suddenly dried up. To make things worse, all the bathroom mirrors had been broken in transit and their replacements still hadn't been installed. Luggage, of course, went astray, but was located and returned only a matter of moments before the new visitors populated the bars and got on with the serious business of enjoying themselves. Fundu Lagoon had come alive as a hotel.

The tone set by this first group was important. Fundu Lagoon would be unlike more traditional hotels and resorts; this place would have the character of its owners firmly embedded in its DNA.

The peaceful, informal luxury created a convivial house party atmosphere. Fundu Lagoon's sophisticated friendly identity was established in that first week. There was also another exciting reason to visit Fundu Lagoon's dreamy shores, as those first visitors discovered.

The diving in and around Pemba is rated as some of the best on the planet. The full extent of this incredibly rich and unique marine habitat was unknown to the Directors when they bought the land, but it was now an important part of the hotel's activities. The diving off nearby Misali is especially rich and varied.

Jules Turner

As Ellis and her team appraised the hotel's performance, it became clear that some of the architectural design needed modification. There was no time to lose. At the end of December, Fundu had to be ready for a very important party. Brian and Ellis would host a week-long event to celebrate the new Millennium.

The restaurant felt too small and it was quickly realised that some of the storerooms were inconveniently located to service a busy hotel. Emma had left two weeks earlier - who could help with the design fine-tune?

Ellis and Marcus pulled Jules Turner aside; would he stay on after the soft opening and work on refining an enlarged restaurant design? His answer was an immediate, "Yes." He took up the challenge and, working closely with the Kenyan roofing contractor Steven, like Emma before him, created the towering scalloped restaurant roof. "I wanted to create curves," Jules said. "We dug the site away and I sat there with my drawing board, pencil and paper and marked out the new area with string." Jules was bowled over by Steven's natural engineering skills; without him the new roof would never have gone up.

The final alterations were completed with less than a week to go before the Millennium party made their way out to Wambaa. It seemed as if everything was now ready, but as guests arrived on the jetty, the generator malfunctioned leaving Fundu Lagoon without power. Again, panic ensued behind the scenes as engineers desperately tried to fire up the temperamental engine. One guest fondly recalls switching the fans on in his room: "If I put the fan on the lights went out, it was such fun!"

There had been much speculation in the media about the Millennium Bug and how it might disrupt the planet. Brian remembers planning the party with great affection. "We were going to watch the Millennium Bug Y2K destroy the world! We'd be safe on the island and watch planes drop out of the sky and cities grind to a halt, but nothing happened!"

Brian and Ellis' invitations brought together a diverse group from all over the world, including film and fashion friends, actors, performance artists and writers, for a week of fun-filled events and activities. By now western attire at the hotel was fully accepted. The staff were proud of their new uniforms and guests could relax in anything from brief beachwear to eccentric floaty chiffon outfits, without offending or alarming.

Daytimes were spent on glorious island hopping trips, village walks, watersports and diving to explore the underwater abundance of beautiful tropical creatures. In the evenings, Ellis and Brian hosted a string of unforgettable dinners and parties.

Fundu staff were as entranced as the guests by spontaneous juggling during meals by circus performers, who tossed exotic fruit into the vaulted ceiling space before deftly returning it undamaged to the diners. Puppeteers transformed napkins into entertaining animated characters. The new and enthusiastic workforce proudly wore Kermit badges given to them by Brian - without knowing who Kermit is!

An inquisitive bush baby got in on the celebrations too and was found in a drunken stupor on the main bar. It became abundantly clear that the local maxim "drunk as a bush baby" had more than a grain of truth to it.

Brian and Ellis' Millennium guests were spellbound, the event had been a wild success. "No one wanted to leave," said Brian. A sentiment shared by the staff who lined up on the jetty and wept as the revellers departed. A feeling of euphoria prevailed - "We did it!"

As the last New Year's Eve guest left, there were other pressing considerations - Fundu Lagoon was now formally open for business. There would be no more rehearsals and trial runs. From now on it was for real.

LEARNING THE ROPES

With the hotel now successfully open, it was time for fine-tuning.

Hannes Wolters

The first key appointment would be that of General Manager. Ellis had her sights on Hannes Wolters, a highly respected manager of the world famous London venue, the Groucho Club. She had known Hannes for many years and had invited him to Fundu. "I knew him to be a kind, loyal and honest person with a huge passion for people and partying!"

Hannes recalls, "Ellis invited me to the Millenium party, during which she asked if I would consider taking on the role. After that I went back to London to hand in my notice and came straight out."

Having already met most of the staff, Hannes was keen to get training underway. "Seventy percent of our staff are from the village community, with no education or job experience. We had, therefore, to hire some key mainland staff who had already been in contact with foreigners. Most of our staff had never seen a white person and so lacked confidence."

Juma Omar Hafidh Kh Machano Hafidh Muhdin Hafidh Kh Machano

Hannes remembers, "All areas needed a lot of attention, but we concentrated first on front of house, kitchen, bar, restaurant and housekeeping."

"None of the local staff had ever been inside a restaurant, so I introduced picture books to make things visual. It took one month alone to perfect laying the tables. So that I could understand where they were coming from, I asked a number of staff to eat with me in the restaurant. What use is a corkscrew if you've never seen a bottle of wine before?! At the beginning none of the local villagers wanted to work in the bar as alcohol is against their religion. Now they are willing to do so with no problem."

"The first chefs didn't understand portion size and order of service. Plates came out from the kitchen in complete disorder, not only by table, but they cooked all fish together, all chicken together and so on, regardless. The portions were the size of Mount Kilimanjaro and I quickly realised why. In the village they would only eat one meal a day, if they could afford it."

"Our first few head chefs we had to let go. They had received the title somewhere, but their attitude and cooking was terrible. From then on we trained our own, including our first Head Chef, Hafidh. I saw potential in him and it worked wonderfully - until he was poached. I guess this backs up our intention to train staff so that they can work anywhere in the world."

"Finding reliable suppliers presented a completely different set of difficulties," Hannes recalls. "The village community didn't deal with money at that time; they were still bartering." When supplies did not turn up, Hannes had to, on occasions, drive around the island in a minivan buying up all the goods he could find in order to feed guests, none of whom were any the wiser. "When things aren't available, you have to be creative. Always have a plan B."

Ongoing development of the kitchen has been key to Fundu's success and Hannes has been instrumental in creating the hotel's locally sourced, organic, multi-national cuisine.

Hatibu Haji Ibrahim

Staff training was not straightforward. "At the beginning I lost my cool and yelled," said Hannes. "It was one of the worst mistakes I made, as they were too fragile and far too afraid to understand. So I learned to be patient and repeat training sessions. Suddenly it clicked. I had to understand these are very proud people and I had to follow certain rules of etiquette when addressing them. Some were older than me, so they needed a great deal of respect."

"As time went on, staff slowly started training each other. This concept was very difficult to get across in the beginning. No one wanted to teach anyone what he knew because that person would become competition. Teamwork wasn't highly regarded."

"Training staff into managerial positions was also problematic. Those who were promoted believed that when they reached a certain position they no longer had to work. So I had to set an example by being around and constantly checking on the quality of their departments' work."

"Working with such a remote society also means you are more than the resort's General Manager. You become brother, father, doctor, teacher, lawyer and you sometimes have to be available 24/7 - and be cool about it."

"Another matter we had to deal with at a later stage was the new introduction of taxes, which the government didn't explain to workers, so we ended up with a riot in the resort over the Christmas period. Everyone stopped work because they thought we were stealing their money, even after we explained that taxes had nothing to do with us. Eventually the Labour Office had to come in and confront the whole workforce."

The relationship between the hotel and the village, like that of its staff, is generally very good, although difficulties can arise when villagers need something. "There is still an idea that there's an endless supply of money here," says Hannes, "and it's a slow, gentle process to make everyone understand that while we do help, we have budgets."

After several memorable years at Fundu, Hannes returned to London. Although he has subsequently managed the resort for a second time.

Clara Riera Roig   Julia Bishop   Katia Wellving

Sele   Fara

During Hannes' employment break and with big shoes to fill, Julia Bishop embraced the role of manager, engaging with the guests, staff and villagers. Her fluent Swahili helped immeasurably. Julia remembers, "It's great watching the famous 'Fundu Factor' kick in with guests - that's the horizontal beach feeling you get here after 24 hours, when you're so blissed-out that you don't care what day it is." After several very happy and productive seasons, working closely with community projects and issues, Julia decided to leave.

Her successors were another remarkable, hard-working management team, Matt Semark and Anie Ardiani, who brought new systems from their previous employment in Indonesia.

Assistant managers Katia Wellving and Jonathan Jeffery were among other highly valued members of staff, all of whom have helped enormously over the hotel's lifetime to make it a success.

Early on in building Fundu Lagoon, an office was established in Stone Town, Unguja. Key staff based there had the responsibility of keeping the resort supplied with a miscellany of essential items ranging from building materials to toothbrushes. Most food and drink also needed to come across to Pemba and when shipping was delayed, fridges and freezers at the office kept meat and fresh food from perishing.

Official documents were also all generated and processed through Stone Town, including land leases, planning permission, work permits and visas, making the office central to the efficient running of the resort.

The Stone Town office is now well managed by loyal employee Sele, who has been with Fundu since the beginning. He works alongside an office administrator, Fara.

Maurice Turner was Fundu Lagoon's first Financial Controller, initially based in Stone Town as there was no internet on Pemba then. It was from this office that he oversaw some of the complicated crucial logistics that help the hotel operate. Maurice remembers the early days fondly. "I saw Fundu develop. It was like a child growing. I spent four amazing years working there, some of the best of my life."

Clara Riera Roig, Financial Controller after Maurice, said, "When I first arrived, I couldn't believe such a place existed. Fundu Lagoon is magical."

Maurice Turner

Rusty and Martie Rauscher

Kessy Mwinshehe

Lizzie Msangi

Two exceptional employees who have given outstanding loyal service to Fundu over many years are Martie and Rusty Rauscher. "Their positive outlook, problem-solving skills and kindness to all people, along with a great sense of humour, made them a perfect fit for the Fundu family," said Ellis. Still employed today, Martie is the current Financial Controller, and her husband Rusty is a highly skilled boat builder, fisherman and maintenance craftsman who oversees keeping everything at the hotel in perfect working order. "When we see guests enjoying themselves, we know we helped make that happen. We work with the best people, but it never feels like work. Who works like this? It makes us feel peaceful."

Many staff have stayed at Fundu since the beginning and their loyalty has produced great results, both for the hotel and for them as individuals.

Kessy's story is typical. He worked in the hotel stores for five years before being promoted to reception and then on to the front office team, before becoming accounts receptionist. Kessy was keen to do more and often assisted with other jobs. He became indispensable and is now a vital member of staff as Front Office Manager. Kessy also deals with village issues, consulting on the village fund and staff tips. His diplomacy is invaluable when dealing with governmental matters, taxes and local permits.

Lizzie's first job was looking after the shop before graduating to reception for a year. Then, after waitressing for another five years, she became the head of the restaurant until her promotion to Assistant Manager. "Some of my colleagues felt resentment and I even thought I should go back to being a waitress until I realised this was a great opportunity."

Filbert Ngenlenge

Craig Sigston   Eric Wear

With its own fully equipped dive facility, the emphasis at Fundu Lagoon is on getting the most out of the sport while retaining total respect for the environment and diver safety. Dive 710 is staffed by an experienced team that has vast knowledge of the local area, and the powerful dive boats ensure that all the sites off Pemba are within easy reach.

Filbert, like everyone else newly arrived on site, helped out with finishing the build, and a couple of days before the first guests arrived he was allotted his new post. He'd be helping out in the Dive Centre, not that he had ever heard about such a department before.

The first Dive Centre Manager, Craig Sigston, took all his new staff out for a trial dive at the end of the jetty. Filbert was immediately hooked, although there was one small, yet important consideration to take into account - he couldn't swim. But he was keen to learn. He subsequently swam every evening and swotted up on the PADI Open Water book. Craig spotted his enthusiasm and suggested that diving might be his future.

The following year Filbert took Advanced Diving and Rescue courses and by 2002 he'd become a Dive Master. Twelve months later an Instructor course was held in Zanzibar for the first time; it was too good an opportunity to miss. Filbert spoke with Ellis, Marcus and Alex, "They said go for it, they encouraged me and said if you fail, then not to worry, at least you tried." Filbert was the only entrant to pass the exam and became the first ever Tanzanian dive instructor. In 2007 Filbert was promoted to running Dive 710.

Filbert's managerial appointment is another great example of Fundu Lagoon's ethos of promoting and supporting local talent.

The rarely dived waters in the Indian Ocean around Pemba are among the richest and most exciting in the world. Shallow coral lagoons drop off to spectacular depths supporting a vast range of marine life, and they provide some of the most exhilarating drift diving and snorkelling in East Africa.

Fundu Lagoon's Dive 710 has now achieved the honour of being a PADI five star resort. It is committed to sharing the thrill and diversity of life in the surrounding seas, whilst conserving this healthy and abundant natural phenomena for future generations.

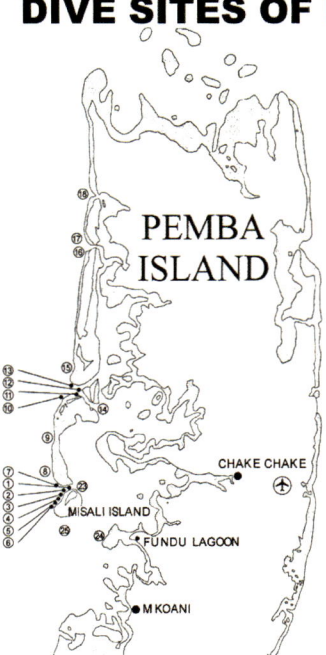

DIVE SITES OF PEMBA

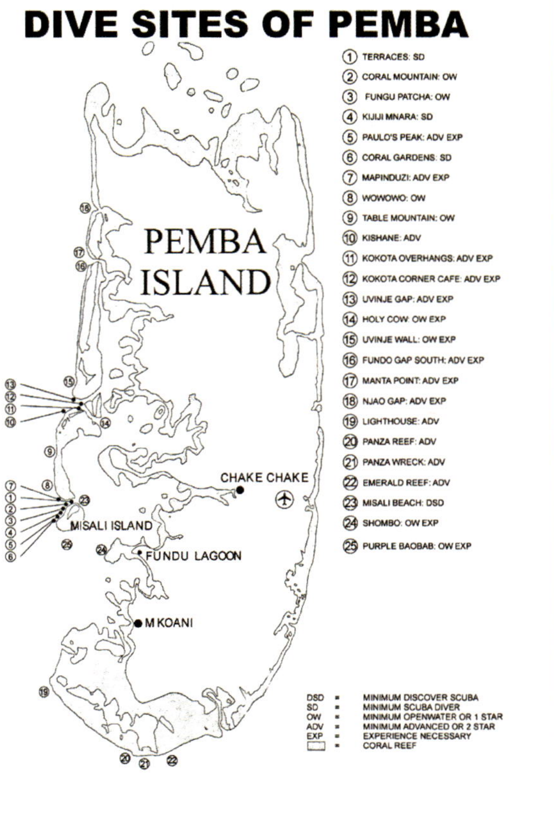

PEMBA ISLAND

① TERRACES: SD
② CORAL MOUNTAIN: OW
③ FUNGU PATCHA: OW
④ KIJIJI MNARA: SD
⑤ PAULO'S PEAK: ADV EXP
⑥ CORAL GARDENS: SD
⑦ MAPINDUZI: ADV EXP
⑧ WOWOWO: OW
⑨ TABLE MOUNTAIN: OW
⑩ KISHANE: ADV
⑪ KOKOTA OVERHANGS: ADV EXP
⑫ KOKOTA CORNER CAFE: ADV EXP
⑬ UVINJE GAP: ADV EXP
⑭ HOLY COW: OW EXP
⑮ UVINJE WALL: OW EXP
⑯ FUNDO GAP SOUTH: ADV EXP
⑰ MANTA POINT: ADV EXP
⑱ NJAO GAP: ADV EXP
⑲ LIGHTHOUSE: ADV
⑳ PANZA REEF: ADV
㉑ PANZA WRECK: ADV
㉒ EMERALD REEF: ADV
㉓ MISALI BEACH: DSD
㉔ SHOMBO: OW EXP
㉕ PURPLE BAOBAB: OW EXP

- CHAKE CHAKE
- MISALI ISLAND
- FUNDU LAGOON
- MKOANI

DSD = MINIMUM DISCOVER SCUBA
SD = MINIMUM SCUBA DIVER
OW = MINIMUM OPENWATER OR 1 STAR
ADV = MINIMUM ADVANCED OR 2 STAR
EXP = EXPERIENCE NECESSARY
▢ = CORAL REEF

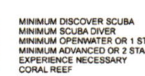

Like the exceptional diving, Pemba offers world-class sport fishing opportunities. Catches include, for example: wahoo, trevally, marlin, sailfish, tuna and dorado. Today Fundu's resident angling expert, Rusty Rauscher, takes guests out on half and whole day trips, during which they might bag prize-winning catches. Most fish are returned safely to the sea, but some are brought back to the hotel and are cooked that evening for dinner or served as sashimi during sundowners in the jetty bar.

Boats are pivotal to the day-to-day running of both the hotel and the Dive Centre. Exploring the neighbouring islands by boat has, since Fundu first opened its doors, been one of the great treats and favourite pastimes of guests. Pods of dolphins and seasonal sightings of whales contribute to these special days.

Dhows are ever present and a romantic sunset cruise on Fundu's own dhow, Mama Casa, is a must.

The acceptance of Fundu Lagoon into the local community is complete. It affords total seclusion to visitors, whilst leaving the local culture and lifestyle undisturbed.

The environmentally friendly style and ethos blends the hotel perfectly into its surroundings. It is a haven for naturalists, where fabulous animal and plant species continue to flourish, uninterrupted by guests coming and going.

Visitors are sometimes treated to very special sightings of the intriguing indigenous creatures that abound in and around Pemba, most famously the Pemba flying fox (large fruit bat), bush baby, blue-balled or velvet monkey and marsh mongoose. There are four endemic bird species only found on Pemba, namely the scops owl, green pigeon, violet breasted sunbird and Pemba white-eye. Other spectacular bird species to spot are hadada, African goshawk, palm-nut vulture and malachite kingfisher, as well as hornbills and many others.

Nearer ground level, rare crabs, geckos, chameleon, butterflies and moths contribute to the rich ecosystem. An endemic plant species is the Pemba palm, known locally as Mapapindi. Further inland much of the vegetation is lush and tropical, earning Pemba its reputation as the Emerald Isle. Exotic fruits and spices abound.

THE DARK SIDE

It's easy to be buoyed along in the joyous fairytale story of Fundu Lagoon, but it is important to place its development in a wider context and understand that creating a venture like this can also have darker, more problematic aspects.

Storm clouds loomed over the project on occasions, and in the early stages of development a series of difficult setbacks threatened to scupper Fundu Lagoon entirely.

Within two months of the hotel opening, Ellis, Marcus and Alex were drawn into crisis talks. An audit confirmed suspicions that there were problems with John Banks' Fundu accounting. Complaints had also been received about bullying and threatening behaviour. After an investigation it was decided that there was no longer a role for John in the management of the hotel.

Soon after Hannes started as General Manager, he too had some difficult times. When the hotel first opened, large amounts of cash were needed to pay staff wages and local suppliers. It was felt the safest place to deal with money was in the Stone Town office; at that time situated out of town in a private house with security guards.

One night, as both Ellis and Hannes slept at the Stone Town house, they were burgled – all the money had been taken. On realising what had happened next morning, they telephoned their good friend and fellow hotelier Emerson Skeens for advice. He was thankful they hadn't woken during the raid for fear the outcome may have been far worse. The next day the Stone Town office moved location.

A police investigation found some of the stolen money hidden under the bed of a security guard who worked at the house. He was jailed and the investigation continued for years, but without successfully finding the other culprits.

Troubles were further compounded by the Zanzibar

elections held in the year 2000. Violence frequently broke out and tourism to the islands plummeted. The timing couldn't have been worse for the fledgling hotel – it lay empty, like all hotels in Zanzibar at the time, just as it needed to build its reputation and welcome paying guests.

Ellis could see that more money was needed if they were to have any chance of survival. The build had gone over-budget, John Banks had left them with debts that compromised Fundu's lines of supply and the local political problems had left the hotel sitting empty. She remembers it as the most challenging time. "We'd finished the project, we were so happy, so in love with everything going on, it all seemed perfect. But these problems very nearly finished us." There wasn't any choice; if they were to get through, they needed reinvestment.

Brian Henson was open to the idea of helping out, so Ellis and Alex travelled to Los Angeles to talk through the hotel's predicament. Brian was a great help; he analysed the problems and introduced new ideas to the table. His business acumen and calm, measured scrutiny was invaluable. "The options were clear," he said, "either the hotel was sold in a fire sale for close to nothing - which would mean the end of it - or Fundu required reinvestment." The troubled Zanzibari political situation didn't feel permanent; they were certain that if they could keep the jungle from consuming the resort, Fundu would have a bright future. Brian agreed to reinvest in the project - Fundu Lagoon would weather the storm.

THE JOURNEY CONTINUES

Getting the hotel up and running and securing a robust financial footing were major achievements, but there was still much to be done.

The beauty of Fundu Lagoon needed to be captured in pictures for brochures and publicity. Ellis' friend, fashion photographer Ken Niven, was just the man for the job. When he set out for the resort he recalled, "I had no idea of where we were going."

Fundu proved to be a photogenic dream. Ken and his assistant spent three weeks shooting the many different aspects of the hotel.

Soon after his arrival a storm blew in and Ken ran down the jetty with his 5 x 4 inch large format 1920's film camera. The weather possessed a special type of magic, which Ken recognised in the glowering black sky, counterbalanced by the setting sun above an ice rink of turquoise water. To this day he says it is one of the best pictures he has ever taken.

This was a time before digital photography was the norm. "There were so many images that I could have taken, but I only had so much film. I could have shot indefinitely! I had to calm down and get off a rollercoaster of visual ecstasy!"

As they were shooting during the political upheaval, the hotel was deserted. "It was surreal," said Ken, "it was like being in a tropical mansion, an equatorial Downton Abbey if you will, that was empty apart from cooks and waiters, with no other guests."

Fundu had made its mark again. "I remember leaving and thinking it was the most incredible three weeks. It's a place to run away to, sit down with your headphones on and listen to 'Wish You Were Here'. That's the sort of hotel I think it is, full of Pink Floyd album covers!"

The Fundu look was still evolving. At the soft opening Ellis spent time with her friend Nigel Scott-Harden, a landscape designer. It was a boon having him on site where they could discuss the options for Fundu's grounds. He understood the structure and architectural value immediately and agreed to take on the job.

In 2001 he returned with Ellis and Neil to see the site, where he set about putting it into order, firstly by removing huge amounts of unwanted scrub. "For the first week all I did was edit, with a hundred men and women carrying rubbish in a long line along the beach, morning till night."

Now he could see what was needed to fit in with the style of the place. "Ellis' taste I knew already, she likes the wild and natural, she doesn't like contrived." Nigel, Ellis, Neil, Patrick and Hamisi, from Fundu's garden department, headed to Mombasa to source new plants.

Finding a palm arboretum was key and their search unearthed many prize specimens such as fishtail, traveller, hurricane and footstool palms. They were keen to buy large trees, but if a plant couldn't be carried by three men then they'd rule it out. They bought palms and a huge amount of tropical plants from a variety of nurseries. Ellis and Neil then returned to Fundu. Now Nigel, Patrick and Hamisi had to figure out how to transport their live cargo.

The men needed a dhow and travelled sixty miles south of Mombasa to source one. The small party reached the sea just as night began to fall, but the dhow they had arranged was not there.

"I can see it now," said Nigel. "A mangrove swamp and a white spit of sand; the decaying struts from sunken boats sticking out from the sand like bones. It was very eerie."

Fortunately, their dhow sailed in the next day and Nigel left Patrick and Hamisi to load it with the delicate cargo while he returned to Pemba to continue his work there, on the understanding that the boat would arrive two days later with the plants. It eventually turned up five days late at five in the evening, after a difficult voyage. "I had to mobilise everyone on site to get the plants off the boat and get them watered. I didn't want them to die!" They survived and were quickly positioned and planted, forming the backbone of Fundu's exotic tropical gardens.

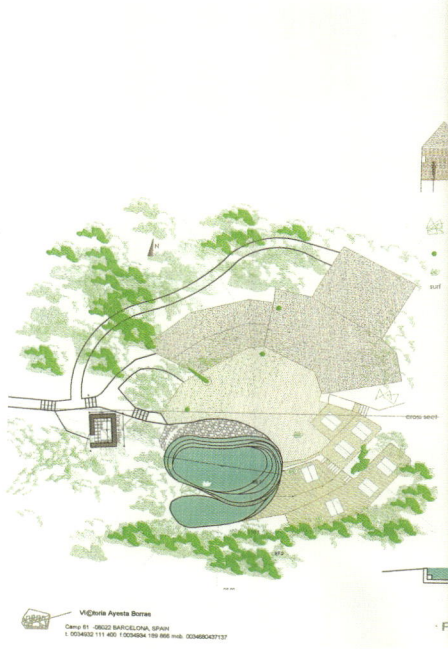

A few years after opening, Fundu's owners bought an adjacent plot of land. This would enable them to spread the bungalows further apart and provide an even greater sense of simple luxury.

Ambitions to create the superior suites were born at this point, and the building of a pool and spa at long last seemed possible.

Architect Victoria Ayesta, or Vito as she's known, first heard about Fundu Lagoon after her twin sister had her honeymoon there. Little did she know that her life would become inextricably involved in the place when she was introduced to Marcus by her twin. She went on to marry him!

Fundu had an immediate effect on Vito. "The jetty and jetty bar impressed me very much - so remote but so inviting, it's like you belong. Instantly you know you could stay forever."

By 2006 budgets allowed for construction work on the pool and spa to begin; Vito would design it. Siting the pool on top of the hill would give it privacy, provide a contrast with the beach, open up stunning views and catch the breeze.

To create the infinity pool, Vito spent many days surveying the area before she decided on the best levels for the decking. An orange sheet was strung up to keep the rain off the twenty two men who took two weeks to dig out the hole by hand. The whole build was completed in a little over two months.

Two large mango trees would provide poolside shade from the intense sun. The infinity effect worked. "The pool connects with the ocean," says Vito proudly. "Its creation is one of the highlights of my life. Fundu Lagoon is so versatile it's possible to do anything. It feels like it's always been there, almost like magic."

The newly purchased beach front adjacent to the pool area proved to be the perfect space for four fabulous super-sized superior suites facing the ocean, each with their own mezzanine leisure platform, private dining area and plunge pool.

Subtle improvements and development to the site continues each year, not least during the rainy season in April, May and June when the hotel closes for refurbishment and maintenance. During these times new creations appear, like Rusty's whimsical beach bar beyond the restaurant.

A BIGGER SPLASH

Fundu Lagoon's impact on visiting guests and those who work there is now well documented, but its reach and influence on the surrounding villages and communities should not be underestimated.

In economic terms, Fundu's footprint is highly significant. It is the largest single employer on Pemba Island, with more than a hundred islanders working at the resort. They in turn support their own extended families, a tradition found throughout African culture. Upwards of a thousand people depend, to a greater or lesser degree, on the salaries that Fundu pays each month.

Social responsibility has always been a core value at Fundu, since Ellis and Marcus promised the Sheha that it would be so at their first meeting. Their promise is evidenced by the Village Fund which has been set up to look after local welfare, and which many of Fundu's guests very generously support. Each of three villages adjacent to Fundu is represented on a steering committee to decide how the money should be spent, with the help and advice of Kessy and the General Manager.

The Fund helps with projects requested by the community as a whole, such as clean water, health and schooling. Today the local villages have wells, electricity and most importantly a mosque.

Fundu guests have helped finance the village school. Local custom dictates that if the walls are constructed, then the government would be obliged to put the roof on. This was also a lesson in self-help. Fundu would supply all the building materials but the village had to provide the labour; the arrangement paid off handsomely.

More fund raising has since been carried out for the school. The most recent efforts have furnished the classrooms with benches and tables.

The project is bearing fruit; over three hundred children attend classes today and several students have passed their exams with flying colours, going on to further education on mainland Tanzania.

Projects like this make positive and permanent developmental changes in the lives of others.

Mama Fatma Ali works in Fundu's housekeeping and like several other employees, she started work at the very beginning. Before Fundu was built, Fatma remembers eking out a living with a little fishing and farming. The houses then were made of mud and lit with candles. She, like others, was wary of this new project, "I was worried that our society was going to change."

To some degree things have changed, but for the better. Many people in the villages have been able to build their own homes using blocks and tin roofs rather than mud. Local cottage industries have sprung up in the community. Fundu continues to have great vision for the benefit of those nearby.

Plans for the next endeavour, construction of a medical centre, are at an early stage, but the village community has given land in preparation for the project.

Even though the medical centre has yet to be built, Fundu has always been there to assist during medical emergencies and often helps transport local people to hospital. The office has become an unofficial clinic for employees and villagers alike. The medicine box is full of rubber gloves, cotton wool, antiseptic, bandages and rehydrating powders.

Equally, Fundu has helped pay for life-transforming operations for several children and youngsters, sending them as far as India for specialist operations. Many children suffering from the effects of rickets and clubfoot and various ophthalmic, dental and congenital malformation problems have had successful treatment.

A co-operative farming venture suffered several false starts, including bad irrigation, unsuitable plots and unscrupulous local landlords. Although, with hard work and steering in the right direction, it has now managed to buy its own land and Fundu has helped finance the costs of a well and imported electricity.

However, this working scheme is there to make a profit. To this end, the co-op intends in the foreseeable future to supply Fundu with all the vegetables they need, as well as selling to other markets. It is really significant, providing an opportunity for people to earn money and lead healthier lives without changing cultural set-ups. This exceptional Wambaa project has been acknowledged internationally.

FUNDU LAGOON AWARDS

The Good Safari Guide Awards:
2016 Winner Best Marine Safari Experience in Africa
2015 Winner Best Marine Safari Experience in Africa
2014 Winner Best Marine Safari Property in Africa
2011 Runner Up Best Beach Safari Property in Africa
2010 Runner Up Best Beach Safari Property in Africa
2009 Winner Best Beach Safari Camp in Africa
2008 Winner Best Beach Safari Property in Africa

Trip Advisor Awards:
2016 Winner Traveller's Choice Hotel Award - Top 1%
2015 Winner Traveller's Choice Hotel Award
2011, 2012, 2013, 2014, 2015 Certificate of Excellence
2011, 2012, 2013, 2014, 2015 Hall of Fame

2015 Luxury Travel Guide Award
Global Awards Winner 2015

THE FINAL WORD

Today, some two decades since Brian and Ellis first visited Stone Town and the idea for a hotel was first mooted, Fundu Lagoon is still welcoming guests. That the place was ever built and continues to flourish is not only due to the inherent magic and beauty of Pemba Island, but also the dogged belief and tenacity of Ellis, Marcus, Alex and Brian. It is also the wonderful achievement of all those past and present who have worked as part of the Fundu family.

PRESS QUOTES 2000 - 2015

Conde Nast Traveller "Flyte's Fantasy." "It took 5 years to find the perfect site and another one to build the resort, but this month fashion designer Ellis Flyte... will open her latest and possibly most ambitious enterprise yet - Fundu Lagoon."

Marie Claire "Take handsome twin brother property developers, a model turned fashion designer and London's exclusive Groucho Club and what have you got? Fundu Lagoon."

The Independent "Groucho Sur Mer."

Harpers & Queen "Free Spirit." "Image of Serenity and peaceful energy."

The Guardian "Fantasy Islands." "The hidden beauty of Fundu Lagoon; it sneaks up on you as you speed across the bay... It is effortless and luxurious in a barefoot sensual way."

Tatler Best Hotels "Designer Ellis Flyte of Flyte Ostell has created an eco-paradise so discreetly landscaped into Pemba Island that initially you think you've arrived in the middle of nowhere."

Hip Hotels - Beach "At Fundu you get two paradises, one above the water and one below. Here you can be Crusoe and Cousteau in the same day."

Dive In Style "This hotel was carved out of the jungle. Fundu is a different kind of resort. Simple yet stylish. It offers real charm and character - and grows on you at an alarming rate."

Vogue Living "Owned by Fashion Designer Ellis Flyte, its 21st century Robinson Crusoe feel is the epitome of shabby chic."

Sunday Telegraph "The closest thing to tropical paradise I've ever visited."

The Telegraph "Fundu Lagoon is the epitome of barefoot chic and has a distinct Robinson Crusoe feel about it."

Net A Porter "Where to go for the ultimate in laid-back luxury."

Daily Mail "Lapping up the love on a wildly romantic African honeymoon."

The Rake "Lush, unfussy and absurdly elegant, Fundu Lagoon will make the visitor think twice before using the term unspoilt about anywhere else on earth."

Island Hotel Stories "The simplicity of this idyllic setting is the work of its Scottish owner, Ellis Flyte, a designer and nomad with an inquisitive and subtle soul, forever dreaming of far away seas and the ideal hideaway."

International Traveller "Forty kilometers off the Tanzanian coast lies an exotic paradise that's a little hard to get to, but even harder to leave."

Telegraph Travel "Dive of a Lifetime. The Island of Pemba offers some of the best underwater adventures in Africa."

The Observer "Fundu is Africa at its most eco-chic."

The Sunday Times Travel "The Greatest Escape. The scent of cloves on the breeze, deserted white-sand beaches, snorkelling off the coral reef - everything you could want from a holiday paradise."

Square Mile Magazine "Every inch of their playground is unspoilt. If Mother Nature made resorts, they would look like Fundu Lagoon."

Elle Lifestyle "Fundu Lagoon, best barefoot luxury."

Green Rooms "The laid-back style cleverly combines the best of African tradition with sustainable local materials and sophisticated hippy chic."

Must fly... must buy

DIVING INTO PARADISE

All aboard for Zanzibar

FASHION designer Ellis Flyte, one half of former label duo Flyte Ostell, has announced plans to open a small, exclusive holiday resort in the ecological paradise of Pemba Island, Zanzibar — described by a spokesperson as "one of the most stunning dive islands in the world". Scheduled to open next summer, the lagoonside resort — aimed at the fashionable "21st century Robinson Crusoe" traveller — will consist of around 20 cabins on stilts in an area rich in coral and marine life. The as-yet-unnamed development will combine "a heavy emphasis on diving and environmental activities", among them wild dolphin-spotting and turtle watching, with a "house-party" feel. Flyte, who spent two years researching and developing her own project "in association with the local government, an environmentalist and other investors", emphasises that her resort has been "designed to cause the minimum environmental disruption", and is supervising the construction process. Local fabrics and textiles will be incorporated in the interior design.

PICTURE CREDITS

Ellis Flyte would especially like to thank photographers Ken Niven, Peter Bennett, Albert Font, Dario Mitidieri and Architect and Designer Victoria (Vito) Ayesta, for the use of their images.

Front cover - Ken Niven

Back cover - original painting by Jake Paltenghi

By page number, left to right and top to bottom:-

1: Carl Swaby, Joseph Armario, Victoria Ayesta, Rob Munro (www.stewartcomms.com) 2: Map by Alison Davies, The Mapping Company 3: Dario Mitidieri 5: Ken Niven 6: Craig T Duncan, Brian Henson x 10 8: Brian Henson 9: Brian Henson 10: Albert Font 11: Ken Niven 13: Ken Niven 14: Ken Niven 15: Directors 16: Mike Neufeld 17: n/c 18: Emma Day (Garstang) x 2 20: Peter Bennett 21: Ellis Flyte 22: Allison Denyer 24: Ken Niven 27: Ken Niven 28: Ellis Flyte x 2 29: Ellis Flyte x 2, Naomi Neufeld 30: Ellis, Directors, Emma Day 31: Emma Day x 2 32: Emma Day 33: Directors x 3 34: Directors x 3 35: Albert Font 36: Vito Ayesta x 4 37: Directors x 4 38: Vito Ayesta x 2, Directors x 5 39: Directors, Vito Ayesta, Directors x 4 40: Emma Day x 2, Vito Ayesta, Emma Day, Vito Ayesta, Directors 41: Vito Ayesta, Directors 42: Vito Ayesta x 2, Ellis Flyte/Directors x 6 43: Ken Niven 44: Ellis Flyte x 3, Ken Niven 45: Neil Pascoe 46: Ellis Flyte, Dario Mitidieri x 2 47: Ellis Flyte x 2 48: Craig T Duncan, Ellis Flyte x 2, Peter Bennett, Ellis Flyte, Craig T Duncan, Ken Niven, Allison Denyer, Ellis Flyte x 2, Craig T Duncan, Peter Bennett 49: Ellis Flyte x 2 50: Ken Niven x 2, Ellis Flyte, Ken Niven x 4, Ellis Flyte, Ken Niven 51: Peter Bennett, Ellis Flyte x 2, Ken Niven x 2, Peter Bennett, Ken Niven, Peter Bennett, Ken Niven 52: Ellis Flyte/Neil Pascoe x 6 53: Ellis Flyte, Vito Ayesta 54: Directors x 3 55: Emma Day 56: Emma Day, Directors 57: Directors x 3, Dario Mitidieri 58: Dario Mitidieri, Directors 59: Albert Font 60: Directors x 5 61: Ken Niven 62: Directors x 4 63: Directors, Ken Niven 64: Ellis Flyte/Neil Pascoe x 6 65: Ellis Flyte/Neil Pascoe x 2 66: Directors x 3 67: Ellis Flyte, Albert Font, Ken Niven 68: Directors x 6 69: Directors x 4 70: Peter Bennett 71: Peter Bennett 72: Ellis Flyte, Dario Mitidieri, Ellis Flyte, Vito Ayesta, Ellis Flyte, Dario Mitidieri, Ellis Flyte 73: Michael Earl 75: Ken Niven 76: Peter Bennett, Directors, Dario Mitidieri, Bronwyn & Jono Earl, Peter Bennett, Craig T Duncan, Ken Niven, Ellis Flyte, Directors, Dario Mitidieri x 2, Peter Bennett, Ellis Flyte 77: Albert Font, Directors, Dario Mitidieri, Directors, Peter Bennett, Hannes Wolters, Ken Niven, Directors, Ellis Flyte, Craig T Duncan x 2, Dario Mitidieri 78: Craig T Duncan 80: Emma Day, Directors 81: Ken Niven 82: Ken Niven 84: Emma Day 85: Ken Niven 86: Peter Bennett 87: Ken Niven 89: Siobhan Quayle 91: Peter Bennett 92: Ken Niven x 36 93: Ken Niven 94: Ken Niven x 2 95: Emma Day 96: Ken Niven x 3 97: Ken Niven x 8 98: Craig T Duncan, Ellis Flyte x 2 99: Ken Niven, Craig T Duncan, Ellis Flyte x 2 100: Peter Bennett, Directors 101: Filbert Nathan Ngelenge x 12 102: Filbert Nathan Ngelenge x 3 103: Ken Niven, Dario Mitidieri, Karen Hymbaugh 104: Craig T Duncan x 2, Martie Rauscher 105: Dario Mitidieri 106: Allison Denyer x 2 107: Archie Brooksbank x 2 (www.bladesmanproductions.com) 109: Craig T Duncan 111: Emma Day 113: William Jima 114: Ken Niven 116: Ellis Flyte x 3 117: Emma Day 118: Vito Ayesta x 6 119: Vito Ayesta x 3, Craig T Duncan 120: Ken Niven 121: Ellis Flyte, Unknown 122: Emma Day, Ellis Flyte x 2 123: Ken Niven 125: Ellis Flyte 126: Peter Bennett, Ellis Flyte, Albert Font 127: Directors, Craig T Duncan, Albert Font, Vito Ayesta, Craig T Duncan, Albert Font, Ken Niven 128: Directors x 3 129: Directors x 4 130: Directors 131: Directors x 4 132: Albert Font, Peter Bennett, Albert Font x 4, Allison Denyer, Mike Neufeld, Albert Font 133: Directors x 4 135: Bronwyn & Jono Earl 138: Ken Niven 141: Peter Bennett 143: Allison Denyer

ACKNOWLEDGEMENTS

A big thank you to all who have shared our equatorial dream. So many evenings over drinks and conversations at the jetty bar where people have said: you could write a book about it, so we have.

As the Visual Director, I would initially like to thank the book people, that is the cast and crew who have helped me from concept to creation:-

Nick, for his imaginative and powerful story-telling.
Alli, for editorial guidance and assistance in all areas.
Ricky, for his dedicated contribution over decades in printing and production.
Special thanks to all of the photographers. I am totally indebted for the striking images over the years.
Craig, for digital processing and picture library assistance.
To Steve Trott and Layne Penrose for facilitating printing and publication.
To the proof readers; Janette Marshall, Judith Jones and Catherine Neufeld for their help and valuable editorial suggestions.

A huge thank you to all those featured and mentioned in the book, whatever part they have played and to all those we have not been able to mention.

And to hoteliers, travellers and friends in India, Malawi, Dar and Zanzibar for their gracious hospitality, advice and assistance.

I am very grateful for the support and co-operation of the Government of Tanzania, officials and lawyers in the preparation of all the required documentation and legal issues for Fundu Lagoon.

Thank you also for the extremely valuable relationships within our local village community.

Grateful thanks to guests who have contributed to our ongoing welfare fund.

Huge appreciation to the wonderful visitors to Fundu who have completed the picture with their celebrations, holidays and goodwill.

Ellis Flyte

THE STORY OF FUNDU LAGOON
Realising The Dream

visit us at www.fundulagoon.com

Concept	Brian Henson
Design and Style	Ellis Flyte
Writer	Nick Maes
Editorial & Layout Asst	Allison Denyer
Digital Processing	Craig Thomas Duncan
Print Liaison	Richard Neufeld

Published by:
Penrose Group
London Road
Staines-upon-Thames
TW18 4JJ
info@penrosegroup.co.uk

© The Jim Henson Company 2016

All rights reserved. No part of this publication may be reproduced, stored in a retrieval system, or transmitted in any form or by any means, electronic, mechanical photocopying or otherwise, without the prior permission of the copyright owners. Nor be otherwise circulated in any form of binding or cover other than that in which it is published and without similar condition being imposed on the subsequent purchaser.

The publishers have taken all reasonable care in compiling this work but cannot accept responsibility for the information derived from third parties, which has been reproduced in good faith.

Every effort has been made to contact and credit the copyright holders of photographs. Any omissions or errors will be corrected in future editions.

ISBN 978-0-9955029-0-1

Printed and bound in Great Britain by Penrose Group
www.penrosegroup.co.uk

Woodland CARBON
www.woodlandcarbon.co.uk
Inv Ref 8230973
Printed on Carbon Captured paper

FUNDU LAGOON

Few fabulous dreams make it to reality.

This book tells how a sequence of events and a collaboration of creative people came together and, against all the odds, designed and built one of the world's most individual, warmly welcoming and environmentally sympathetic hotels.